"十四五"职业教育国家规划教材

民航客舱实用英语口语教程（下册）

主　编◎李姝　王莹
副主编◎闫品　陈妍　曹璐璐

Practical English Speaking Course for Aviation Service
（Volume Two）

清华大学出版社
北京

内容简介

《民航客舱实用英语口语教程（下册）》共6单元。每单元均包含核心关键词、热点句型、情景对话和相关文化背景赏析等内容。本教材以搭乘航班的基本流程为主线，较翔实地介绍了在机场、机舱及飞机飞行过程中，空乘服务的常用对话、必备经典句型和民航乘务人员职业文化素养常识，包括机上娱乐、餐饮服务、机上免税服务、紧急状况、中转服务、机场海关移民局检疫等专业场景。

本书封面贴有清华大学出版社防伪标签，无标签者不得销售。
版权所有，侵权必究。举报：010-62782989，beiqinquan@tup.tsinghua.edu.cn。

图书在版编目（CIP）数据

民航客舱实用英语口语教程. 下册 / 李姝，王莹主编. —北京：清华大学出版社，2021.3（2025.2 重印）
"十三五"全国高等院校民航服务专业规划教材
ISBN 978-7-302-57129-2

I. ①民… II. ①李… ②王… III. ①民用航空—乘务人员—英语—口语—高等学校—教材 IV. ①F560.9

中国版本图书馆CIP数据核字（2020）第259582号

责任编辑：杜春杰
封面设计：刘 超
版式设计：文森时代
责任校对：马军令
责任印制：沈 露

出版发行：清华大学出版社
网　　址：https://www.tup.com.cn, https://www.wqxuetang.com
地　　址：北京清华大学学研大厦 A 座　　邮　　编：100084
社 总 机：010-83470000　　邮　　购：010-62786544
投稿与读者服务：010-62776969, c-service@tup.tsinghua.edu.cn
质量反馈：010-62772015, zhiliang@tup.tsinghua.edu.cn

印 装 者：三河市龙大印装有限公司
经　　销：全国新华书店
开　　本：185mm×260mm　　印　张：7　　字　数：230千字
版　　次：2021年3月第1版　　印　次：2025年2月第3次印刷
定　　价：29.80元

产品编号：077342-01

"十三五"全国高等院校民航服务专业规划教材
丛书主编及专家指导委员会

丛 书 总 主 编　　刘　永（北京中航未来科技集团有限公司董事长兼总裁）
丛 书 副 总 主 编　　马晓伟（北京中航未来科技集团有限公司常务副总裁）
丛 书 副 总 主 编　　郑大地（北京中航未来科技集团有限公司教学副总裁）
丛 书 总 主 审　　朱益民（原海南航空公司总裁、原中国货运航空公司总裁、原上海航空公司总裁）
丛 书 英 语 总 主 审　　王　朔（美国雪城大学、纽约市立大学巴鲁克学院双硕士）
丛 书 总 顾 问　　沈泽江（原中国民用航空华东管理局局长）
　　　　　　　　　汪光弟（原上海虹桥国际机场副总裁）
丛 书 总 执 行 主 编　　王益友［江苏民航职业技术学院（筹）院长、教授］
丛 书 艺 术 总 顾 问　　万峻池（美术评论家、著名美术品收藏家）
丛书总航空法律顾问　　程　颖（荷兰莱顿大学国际法研究生、全国高职高专"十二五"规划教材《航空法规》主审、中国东方航空股份有限公司法律顾问）

丛书专家指导委员会主任

　　　　　　　　关云飞（长沙航空职业技术学院教授）
　　　　　　　　张树生（国务院津贴获得者，山东交通学院教授）
　　　　　　　　刘岩松（沈阳航空航天大学教授）
　　　　　　　　宋兆宽（河北传媒学院教授）
　　　　　　　　姚　宝（上海外国语大学教授）
　　　　　　　　李剑峰（山东大学教授）
　　　　　　　　孙福万（国家开放大学教授）
　　　　　　　　张　威（沈阳师范大学教授）
　　　　　　　　成积春（曲阜师范大学教授）

"十三五"全国高等院校民航服务专业规划教材编委会

主　任　高　宏（沈阳航空航天大学教授）　　杨　静（中原工学院教授）
　　　　　李　勤（南昌航空大学教授）　　　　　李广春（郑州航空工业管理学院教授）
　　　　　安　萍（沈阳师范大学）　　　　　　　彭圣文（长沙航空职业技术学院）
　　　　　陈文华（上海民航职业技术学院）

副主任　兰　琳（长沙航空职业技术学院）　　庞庆国（中国成人教育协会航空服务教育培训专业委员会）
　　　　　郑　越（长沙航空职业技术学院）　　郑大莉（中原工学院信息商务学院）
　　　　　徐爱梅（山东大学）　　　　　　　　黄　敏（南昌航空大学）
　　　　　韩　黎［江苏民航职业技术学院（筹）］　曹娅丽（南京旅游职业学院）
　　　　　胡明良（江南影视艺术职业学院）　　李楠楠（江南影视艺术职业学院）
　　　　　王昌沛（曲阜师范大学）　　　　　　何蔓莉（湖南艺术职业学院）
　　　　　孙东海（江苏新东方艺先锋传媒学校）　戴春华（原同济大学）
　　　　　施　进（盐城航空服务职业学校）　　孙　梅（上海建桥学院）
　　　　　张号全（武汉商贸职业学院）　　　　周孟华（上海东海学院）

委　员（排名不分先后）
　　　　　于海亮（沈阳师范大学）　　　　　　于晓风（山东大学）
　　　　　王丽蓉（南昌航空大学）　　　　　　王玉娟（南昌航空大学）
　　　　　王　莹（沈阳师范大学）　　　　　　王建惠（陕西职业技术学院）
　　　　　王　姝（北京外航服务公司）　　　　王　晶（沈阳航空航天大学）
　　　　　邓丽君（西安航空职业技术学院）　　车树国（沈阳师范大学）
　　　　　龙美华（岳阳市湘北女子职业学校）　石　慧（南昌航空大学）
　　　　　付砚然（湖北襄阳汽车职业技术学院，原海南航空公司乘务员）
　　　　　朱茫茫（潍坊职业学院）　　　　　　田　宇（沈阳航空航天大学）
　　　　　刘　洋（濮阳工学院）　　　　　　　刘　超（华侨大学）
　　　　　许　赟（南京旅游职业学院）　　　　刘　舒（江西青年职业学院）
　　　　　杨志慧（长沙航空职业技术学院）　　吴立杰（沈阳航空航天大学）
　　　　　李长亮（张家界航空工业职业技术学院）　杨　莲（马鞍山职业技术学院）
　　　　　李雯艳（沈阳师范大学）　　　　　　李芙蓉（长沙航空职业技术学院）
　　　　　李　仟（天津中德应用技术大学，原中国南方航空公司乘务员）
　　　　　李霏雨（原中国国际航空公司乘务员）　李　姝（沈阳师范大学）
　　　　　邹　昊（南昌航空大学）　　　　　　狄　娟（上海民航职业技术学院）
　　　　　宋晓宇（湖南艺术职业学院）　　　　邹　莎（湖南信息学院）
　　　　　张　进（三峡旅游职业技术学院）　　张　驰（沈阳航空航天大学）
　　　　　张　琳（北京中航未来科技集团有限公司）　张　利（北京中航未来科技集团有限公司）
　　　　　张媛媛（山东信息职业技术学院）　　张程垚（湖南民族职业学院）
　　　　　陈烜华（上海民航职业技术学院）　　陈　卓（长沙航空职业技术学院）
　　　　　周佳楠（上海应用技术大学）　　　　金　恒（西安航空职业技术学院）
　　　　　郑菲菲（南京旅游职业学院）　　　　周茗慧（山东外事翻译职业学院）
　　　　　胥佳明（大连海事大学）　　　　　　赵红倩（上饶职业技术学院）
　　　　　柳　武（湖南流通创软科技有限公司）　胡　妮（南昌航空大学）
　　　　　柴　郁（江西航空职业技术学院）　　钟　科（长沙航空职业技术学院）
　　　　　唐　珉（桂林航天工业学院）　　　　倪欣雨（斯里兰卡航空公司空中翻译，原印度尼西亚鹰航乘务员）
　　　　　高　青（山西旅游职业学院）　　　　高　熔（原沈阳航空航天大学继续教育学院）

郭雅萌（江西青年职业学院）　　高　琳（济宁职业技术学院）
黄　晨（天津交通职业学院）　　黄春新（沈阳航空航天大学）
黄紫葳（抚州职业技术学院）　　黄婵芸（原中国东方航空公司乘务员）
崔祥建（沈阳航空航天大学）　　曹璐璐（中原工学院）
梁向兵（上海民航职业技术学院）崔　媛（张家界航空工业职业技术学院）
彭志雄（湖南艺术职业学院）　　梁　燕（郴州技师学院）
操小霞（重庆财经职业学院）　　蒋焕新（长沙航空职业技术学院）
庞　敏（上海民航职业技术学院）李艳伟（沈阳航空航天大学）

出 版 说 明

随着经济的稳步发展，我国已经进入经济新常态的阶段，特别是十九大指出：当前中国社会的主要矛盾已经转化为人民日益增长的美好生活需要和不平衡不充分的发展之间的矛盾，这客观上要求社会服务系统要完善升级。作为公共交通运输的主要组成部分，民航运输在满足人们对美好生活的追求和促进国民经济发展中扮演着重要的角色，具有广阔的发展空间。特别是"十三五"期间，国家高度重视民航业的发展，将民航业作为推动我国经济社会发展的重要战略产业，预示着我国民航业将会有更好、更快的发展。从国产化飞机 C919 的试飞，到宽体飞机规划的出台，以及民航发展战略的实施，标志着我国民航业已经步入崭新的发展阶段，这一阶段的特点是以人才为核心，而这一发展模式必将进一步对民航人才质量提出更高的要求。面对民航业发展对人才培养提出的挑战，培养服务于民航业发展的高质量人才，不仅需要转变人才培养观念，创新教育模式，更需要加强人才培养过程中基本环节的建设，而教材建设就是其首要的任务。

我国民航服务专业的学历教育，经过 18 年的探索与发展，其在办学水平、办学结构、办学规模、办学条件和师资队伍等方面都发生了巨大的变化，专业建设水平稳步提高，适应民航发展的人才培养体系初步形成。但我们应该清醒地看到，目前我国民航服务类专业的人才培养仍存在着诸多问题，特别是专业人才培养质量仍不能适应民航发展对人才的需求，人才培养的规模与高质量人才短缺的矛盾仍很突出。而目前相关专业教材的开发还处于探索阶段，缺乏系统性与规范性。已出版的民航服务类专业教材，在吸收民航服务类专业研究成果方面做出了有益的尝试，涌现出不同层次的系列教材，推动了民航服务的专业建设与人才培养，但从总体来看，民航服务类教材的建设仍落后于民航业对专业人才培养的实践要求，教材建设已成为相关人才培养的瓶颈。这就需要我们以引领和服务专业发展为宗旨，系统总结民航服务实践经验与教学研究成果，开发全面反映民航服务职业特点、符合人才培养规律和满足教学需要的系统性专业教材，积极有效地推进民航服务专业人才的培养工作。

基于上述思考，编委会经过两年多的实际调研与反复论证，在广泛征询民航业内专家的意见与建议、总结我国民航服务类专业教育的研究成果后，结合我国民航服务业的发展趋势，致力于编写出一套系统的、具有一定权威性和实用性的民航服务类系列教材，为推进我国民航服务人才的培养尽微薄之力。

本系列教材由沈阳航空航天大学、南昌航空大学、郑州航空工业管理学院、上海民航职业技术学院、长沙航空职业技术学院、西安航空职业技术学院、中原工学院、上海外国语大学、山东大学、大连外国语大学、沈阳师范大学、曲阜师范大学、湖南艺术职业学院、陕西师范大学、兰州大学、云南大学、四川大学、湖南民族职业学院、江西青年职业学院、天津交通职业学院、潍坊职业学院、南京旅游职业学院等多所高校的众多资深专家和学者共同打造，还邀请了多名原中国东方航空公司、原中国南方航空公司、原中国国际航空公司和原海南航空公司中从事多年乘务工作的乘务长和乘务员参与教材的编写。

目前，我国民航服务类的专业教育呈现多元化、多层次的办学格局，各类学校的办学模式也呈现出个性化的特点，在人才培养体系、课程设置以及课程内容等方面，各学校之间存在着一定的差异，对教材也有不同的需求。为了能够更好地满足不同办学层次、教学模式对教材的需要，本套教材主要突出以下特点：

第一，兼顾本、专科不同培养层次的教学需要。鉴于近些年我国本科层次民航服务专业办学规模的不断扩大，在教材需求方面显得十分迫切，同时，专科层面的办学已经到了规模化的阶段，完善与更新教材体系和内容迫在眉睫，本套教材充分考虑了各类办学层次的需要，本着"求同存异、个性单列、内容升级"的原则，通过教材体系的科学架构和教材内容的层次化，达到兼顾民航服务类本、专科不同层次教学之需要。

第二，将最新实践经验和专业研究成果融入教材。服务类人才培养是系统性问题，具有很强的内在规定性，民航服务的实践经验和专业建设成果是教材的基础，本套教材以丰富理论、培养技能为主，力求夯实服务基础，培养服务职业素质，将实践层面行之有效的经验与民航服务类人才培养规律的研究成果有效融合，以提高教材对人才培养的有效性。

第三，落实素质教育理念，注重服务人才培养。习近平总书记在党的十九大报告中强调，"要全面贯彻党的教育方针，落实立德树人根本任务，发展素质教育，推进教育公平，培养德智体美全面发展的社会主义建设者和接班人"，人才以德为先，以社会主义价值观铸就人的灵魂，才能使人才担当重任，这也是高校人才培养的基本任务。教育实践表明，素质是人才培养的基础，也是人才职业发展的基石，人才的能力与技能附着在精神与灵魂，但在传统的民航服务教材体系中，包含素质教育板块的教材较为少见。根据党的教育方针，本套教材的编写考虑到素质教育与专业能力培养的关系，以及素质对职业生涯的潜在影响，首次在我国民航服务专业教学中提出专业教育与人文素质并重、素质决定能力的培养理念，以独特的视野，精心打造素质教育教材板块，使教材体系更加系统，强化了教材特色。

第四，必要的服务理论与专业能力培养并重。调研分析表明，忽视服务理论与人文素质所培养出的人才很难有宽阔的职业胸怀与职业精神，其未来的职业生涯发展就会乏力。因此，教材不应仅是对单纯技能的阐述与训练指导，更应该在不淡化专业能力培养的同时，强化行业知识、职业情感、服务机理、职业道德等关系到职业发展潜力的要素的培养，以期培养出高层次和高质量的民航服务人才。

第五，架构适合未来发展需要的课程体系与内容。民航服务具有很强的国际化特点，而我国民航服务的思想、模式与方法也正处于不断创新的阶段，紧紧把握未来民航服务的发展趋势，提出面向未来的解决问题的方案，是本套教材的基本出发点和应该承担的责任。我们力图将未来民航服务的发展趋势、服务思想、服务模式创新、服务理论体系以及服务管理等内容重新进行架构，以期能对我国民航服务人才培养，乃至整个民航服务业的发展起到引领作用。

第六，扩大教材的种类，使教材的选择更加宽泛。鉴于我国目前尚缺乏民航服务专业更高层次办学模式的规范，各学校的人才培养方案各具特点，差异明显，为了使教材更适用于办学的需要，本套教材打破了传统教材的格局，通过课程分割、内容优化和课外外延化等方式，增加了教材体系的课程覆盖面，使不同办学层次、关联专业可以通过教材合理组合，以获得完整的专业教材选择机会。

本套教材规划出版品种大约为四十种，分为：① 人文素养类教材，包括《大学语文》《应用文写作》《艺术素养》《跨文化沟通》《民航职业修养》《中国传统文化》等。② 语言类教材，包括《民航客舱服务英语教程》《民航客舱实用英语口语教程》《民航实用英语听力教程》《民航播音训练》《机上广播英语》《民航服务沟通技巧》等。③ 专业类教材，包括《民航概论》《民航服务概论》《中国民航常飞客源国概况》《民航危险品运输》《客舱安全管理与应急处置》《民航安全检查技术》《民航服务心理学》《航空运输地理》《民航服务法律实务与案例教程》等。④ 职业形象类教材，包括《空乘人员形体与仪态》《空乘人员职业形象设计与化妆》《民航体能训练》等。⑤ 专业特色类教材，包括《民航服务手语训练》《空乘服务专业导论》《空乘人员求职应聘面试指南》《民航面试英语教程》等。

为了开发职业能力，编者联合有关 VR 开发公司开发了一些与教材配套的手机移动端 VR 互动资源，学生可以利用这些资源体验真实场景。

本套教材是迄今为止民航服务类专业较为完整的教材系列之一，希望能借此为我国民航服务人才的培养，乃至我国民航服务水平的提高贡献力量。民航发展方兴未艾，民航教育任重道远，为民航服务事业发展培养高质量的人才是各类人才培养部门的共同责任，相信集民航教育的业内学者、专家之共同智慧，凝聚有识之士心血的这套教材的出版，对加速我国民航服务专业建设、完善人才培养模式、优化课程体系、丰富教学内容，以及加强师资队伍建设能起到一定的推动作用。在教材使用的过程中，我们真诚地希望听到业内专家、学者批评的声音，收到广大师生的反馈意见，以利于进一步提高教材的水平。

丛 书 序

《礼记·学记》曰:"古之王者,建国君民,教学为先。"教育是兴国安邦之本,决定着人类的今天,也决定着人类的未来。企业发展也大同小异,重视人才是企业的成功之道,别无二选。航空经济是现代经济发展的新趋势,是当今世界经济发展的新引擎。民航是经济全球化的主流形态和主导模式,是区域经济发展和产业升级的驱动力。发展中的中国民航业有巨大的发展潜力,其发展战略的实施必将成为我国未来经济发展的增长点。

"十三五"正值实现我国民航强国战略构想的关键时期,"一带一路"倡议方兴未艾,"空中丝路"越来越宽阔。高速发展的民航运输业需要持续的创新与变革,同时,基于民航运输对安全性和规范性要求比较高的特点,其对人才有着近乎苛刻的要求,只有人才培养先行,夯实人才基础,才能抓住国家战略转型与产业升级的巨大机遇,实现民航运输发展的战略目标。我国民航服务人才发展经历多年的积累,建立了较为完善的民航服务人才培养体系,培养了大量服务民航发展的各类人才,保证了我国民航运输业的高速持续发展。与此同时,我国民航人才培养正面临新的挑战,既要通过教育创新提升人才品质,又需要人才培养过程精细化,把人才培养目标落实到人才培养的过程中,而教材作为专业人才培养的基础,需要先行,以发挥引领作用。教材建设发挥的作用并不局限于专业教育本身,其对行业发展的引领。专业人才培养方向的把握,人才素质、知识、能力结构的塑造以及职业发展潜力的培养具有不可替代的作用。

我国民航运输发展的实践表明,人才培养决定着民航发展的水平,而民航人才的培养需要社会各方面的共同努力。我们惊喜地看到,清华大学出版社秉承"自强不息,厚德载物"的人文精神,发挥品牌优势,投身于民航服务专业系列教材的开发,改变了民航服务教材研发的格局,体现了其对社会责任的担当。

本套教材组织严谨,精心策划,高屋建瓴,深入浅出,具有突出的特色。第一,从民航服务人才培养的全局出发,关注了民航服务产业的未来发展趋势,架构了以培养目标为导向的教材体系与内容结构,比较全面地反映了服务人才培养趋势,起到了良好的统领作用;第二,使教材的本质——适用性得到了回归,体现在每本教材均有独特的视角和编写立意,既有高度的提升、理论的升华,也注重教育要素在课程体系中的细化,具有较强的可用性;第三,引入了职业素质教育的理念,补齐了服务人才素质教育缺少教材的短板,可谓对传统服务人才培养理念的一次冲击;第四,教材编写人员参与面非常广泛,这反映出本套教材充分体现了当今民航服务专业教育的教学成果和编写者的思考,形成了相互交流的良性机制,势必会对全国民航服务类专业的发展起到推动作用。

教材建设是专业人才培养的基础,其与教材服务的行业的发展交互作用,共同实现人才培养—社会检验的良性循环,是助推民航服务人才培养的动力。希望这套教材能够在民航服务类专业人才培养的实践中,发挥更积极的作用。相信通过不断总结与完善,这套教材一定会成为具有自身特色的、适应我国民航业发展要求并深受读者喜欢的规范教材。

原海南航空公司总裁、原中国货运航空公司总裁、原上海航空公司总裁

朱益民

2017年9月

前　言

　　高质量空乘服务人才的培养需要建立在科学的培养模式、学科建设、规范的课程体系以及合理的课程内容与有效的教学方法的基础上。本套教材基于空乘工作中常用的语言、语境和所涉及的文化背景编写，旨在提升空乘人员综合素质和能力，是一套立体化的实用教材，力图在教材的科学性、前瞻性和实用性方面有所创新，使本套教材在未来的专业建设与人才培养方面能发挥更大的作用。

　　本教材专门为空中乘务、民航服务、空中商务专业的学生以及有志于从事航空服务业工作的学习者量身打造，内容涉及机场和机舱的乘务工作领域，依据工作流程，配有语言语境及文化背景的相关介绍。本教材共 6 个单元，每单元包含核心关键词、热点句型、情景对话和相关文化背景赏析等模块，以搭乘航班飞行过程中的基本服务流程为主线，较翔实地介绍了在飞机飞行过程中及机场海关检查等环节所涉及的空乘服务工作常用的对话和必备经典句型以及民航乘务人员职业文化常识。

　　本着实用为主、适用为度的原则，从听、说、读、写、译全方位培养学生的英语能力与水平，正是本书的编写原则与宗旨。

　　由于作者水平有限，难免存在不足之处，恳请专家和读者不吝指正，以便内空更加完善。

编　者
2020 年 4 月

CONTENTS 目录

Unit 7　In-flight Entertainment ································· 1
  7.1 Introduction ··· 2
    7.1.1 Language Points and Useful Sentence Patterns ············· 2
    7.1.2 Dialogues ··· 3
    7.1.3 Cultural Background ··· 3
  7.2 Movies ··· 4
    7.2.1 Language Points and Useful Sentence Patterns ············· 4
    7.2.2 Dialogues ··· 5
    7.2.3 Cultural Background ··· 6
  7.3 Music ··· 7
    7.3.1 Language Points and Useful Sentence Patterns ············· 7
    7.3.2 Dialogues ··· 8
    7.3.3 Cultural Background ··· 8
  7.4 Games ··· 9
    7.4.1 Language Points and Useful Sentence Patterns ············· 9
    7.4.2 Dialogues ··· 10
    7.4.3 Cultural Background ··· 10
  7.5 Flight Parameters ··· 11
    7.5.1 Language Points and Useful Sentence Patterns ············· 11
    7.5.2 Dialogues ··· 12
    7.5.3 Cultural Background ··· 13
  7.6 Business and First Class ··· 13
    7.6.1 Language Points and Useful Sentence Patterns ············· 13
    7.6.2 Dialogues ··· 14
    7.6.3 Cultural Background ··· 15

Unit 8　Meal and Drink Service ································· 17

	8.1	Meal Service	18
		8.1.1 Language Points and Useful Sentence Patterns	18
		8.1.2 Dialogues	19
		8.1.3 Cultural Background	19
	8.2	Drinks Service	20
		8.2.1 Language Points and Useful Sentence Patterns	20
		8.2.2 Dialogues	21
		8.2.3 Cultural Background	22
	8.3	Children and Senior People	23
		8.3.1 Language Points and Useful Sentence Patterns	23
		8.3.2 Dialogues	24
		8.3.3 Cultural Background	24
	8.4	Cockpit Catering	25
		8.4.1 Language Points and Useful Sentence Patterns	25
		8.4.2 Dialogues	26
		8.4.3 Cultural Background	26
	8.5	Customs of Different Countries	27
		8.5.1 Language Points and Useful Sentence Patterns	27
		8.5.2 Dialogues	28
		8.5.3 Cultural Background	29
	8.6	Dining Etiquette	29
		8.6.1 Language Points and Useful Sentence Patterns	29
		8.6.2 Dialogues	30
		8.6.3 Cultural Background	31
Unit 9	**Duty-free Sales**		**33**
	9.1	Enquiring In-flight Duty-free Sales	34
		9.1.1 Language Points and Useful Sentence Patterns	34
		9.1.2 Dialogues	35
		9.1.3 Cultural Background	36
	9.2	Buying a present	37
		9.2.1 Language Points and Useful Sentence Patterns	37
		9.2.2 Dialogues	38
		9.2.3 Cultural Background	40
	9.3	Choosing something for oneself	41
		9.3.1 Language Points and Useful Sentence Patterns	41
		9.3.2 Dialogues	42

		9.3.3	Cultural Background	44
	9.4	Duty-Free Allowances		46
		9.4.1	Language Points and Useful Sentence Patterns	46
		9.4.2	Dialogues	47
		9.4.3	Cultural Background	48
	9.5	Preorder Duty-free Products on Board		48
		9.5.1	Language Points and Useful Sentence Patterns	48
		9.5.2	Dialogues	49
		9.5.3	Cultural Background	51

Unit 10　Emergency Situations　53

	10.1	Irregular Flight		54
		10.1.1	Language Points and Useful Sentence Patterns	54
		10.1.2	Dialogues	55
		10.1.3	Cultural Background	56
	10.2	Experiencing Turbulence		59
		10.2.1	Language Points and Useful Sentence Patterns	59
		10.2.2	Dialogues	60
		10.2.3	Cultural Background	62
	10.3	Sick Passengers on Board		64
		10.3.1	Language Points and Useful Sentence Patterns	64
		10.3.2	Dialogues	65
		10.3.3	Cultural Background	67
	10.4	Alternative landing		68
		10.4.1	Language Points and Useful Sentence Patterns	68
		10.4.2	Dialogues	69
		10.4.3	Cultural Background	70

Unit 11　Transfer Service　73

	11.1	Transferring Guidance		74
		11.1.1	Language Points and Useful Sentence Patterns	74
		11.1.2	Dialogues	75
		11.1.3	Cultural Background	76
	11.2	At the Transfer Counter		77
		11.2.1	Language Points and Useful Sentence Patterns	77
		11.2.2	Dialogues	78
		11.2.3	Cultural Background	79

11.3　Missing the Transfer Flight ································ 80
　　11.3.1　Language Points and Useful Sentence Patterns ················ 80
　　11.3.2　Dialogues ································ 81
　　11.3.3　Cultural Background ································ 82

Unit 12　Customs, Immigration and Quarantine ································ 83

12.1　Going through Customs ································ 84
　　12.1.1　Language Points and Useful Sentence Patterns ················ 84
　　12.1.2　Dialogues ································ 85
　　12.1.3　Cultural Background ································ 86
12.2　Going through Immigration ································ 86
　　12.2.1　Language Points and Useful Sentence Patterns ················ 86
　　12.2.2　Dialogues ································ 87
　　12.2.3　Cultural Background ································ 88
12.3　Quarantine Inspection ································ 89
　　12.3.1　Language Points and Useful Sentence Patterns ················ 89
　　12.3.2　Dialogues ································ 90
　　12.3.3　Cultural Background ································ 92

References ································ 93

Unit 7
In-flight Entertainment

7.1 Introduction

Narrow-Body Aircraft
IFE introduction on domestic and regional flights
Wide-Body Aircraft
IFE introduction on long range flights

7.1.1 Language Points and Useful Sentence Patterns

7.1.1.1 Language Points

1. arrange

to put a group of things or people into a correct or suitable sequence, or position

2. contrast

to set off in contrast; compare or appraise in respect to differences

3. occasional

of or relating to a particular occasion; happening sometimes but not often or regularly

4. aisle

a passage (as in a theater, aircraft or train) separating sections of seats

5. fuselage

the central body portion of an aircraft designed to carry the crew and the passengers or cargo

6. accommodate

to provide someone with something desired, needed, or suited

7. diameter

a straight line passing through the center of a figure or body

8. comparison

a statement that someone or something is like someone or something else

9. revenue

the total income produced by a given source

10. factor

one who acts or transacts business for another

7.1.1.2 Useful Sentence Patterns

Could you please give me an earphone?
How can I switch on the screen?
Would you help me turn the voice up?
May I switch a seat because my screen is broken?

Can you teach me how to use this entertainment system?
How Can I use the controller to play the game here?
What should I do if the entertainment doesn't work?
When can I connect the Wi-Fi on board?
Where should I plug in the earphone?
I will help you open it.
There you go!
You can read the instruction here.
Let me help you.

7.1.2 Dialogues

(P: Passenger   A: Attendant)

P: What is a wide-body aircraft?

A: The aircraft with two aisles is a wide-body aircraft.

P: So what's the difference from the narrow-body aircraft?

A: Normally, the wide-body aircraft is used for long distance flight or some domestic line with high passenger flow.

P: Oh, I see.

P: What can I do with the IFE?

A: The IFE can play games, listen to music, and watch movies to help the passengers spend the boring time.

P: Oh, so what is the history of the IFE?

A: It started from 1921, but the form was very simple at that time.

7.1.3 Cultural Background

Narrow-body Aircraft and Wide-body Aircraft

A narrow-body aircraft or single-aisle aircraft has 3～6 seats per row with a sing aisle and a diameter of below 4 meters of width. In contrast, a wide-body aircraft is a larger airliner usually configured with multiple aisles and a fuselage diameter of more than 5 meters and up to 10 seats with two aisles and often provides more travel classes. For the flight length, narrow-body aircrafts are typically the Airbus A320 and Boeing 737, which usually cover short distance flight tasks.

In-flight entertainment (IFE) refers to the entertainment available to aircraft passengers during a flight. In 1936, the airship Hindenburg offered passengers a piano, a lounge, a dining room, a smoking room, and a bar during the 2.5 day flight between Europe and America. After World War II, IFE was delivered in the form of food and drink services, along with an occasional started movie during lengthy flights. In 1985 the first personal audio player was offered to passengers, along with noise cancelling headphones in 1989. During the 1990s, the demand for better IFE was a major factor in the design of aircraft cabins.

A wide-body aircraft, also known as a twin-aisle aircraft, is a jet airliner with a fuselage wide enough to accommodate two passenger aisles with seven or more seats per row. The typical fuselage diameter is 5 to 6 m. In the typical wide-body economy cabin, passengers are seated seven to ten abreast, allowing a total capacity of 200 to 850 passengers. The largest wide-body aircraft are over 6 m wide, and can accommodate up to eleven passengers abreast in high-density configurations.

By comparison, a typical narrow-body airliner has a diameter of 3 to 4 m, with a single aisle, and seats between 3 to 6 per row.

Wide-body aircraft were originally designed for a combination of use efficiency and passenger comfort and also to increase the amount of cargo space. However, airlines quickly gave up to economic factors, and reduced the extra passenger space in order to maximize profits.

7.2　Movies

7.2.1　Language Points and Useful Sentence Patterns

7.2.1.1　Language points

1. related

   directly relating to the subject or problem being discussed or considered

2. distribute

   to share things among a group of people

3. commence

   to begin or start something

4. cabin

   an area inside a plane where the passengers sit or where the pilot works

5. situated

   having a site in a particular place or position

6. channel

   a television station and all the programmes that it broadcasts

7. broadcast

   to send out radio or television programmes

8. affair

   commercial, professional, public, or personal business

9. stream

if you steam sound or video, you play it on your computer while it is being DOWNLOADED from the Internet, rather than saving it as a FILE and the playing it

7.2.1.2 Useful Sentence Patterns

How can I start a movie?
Should I select a comedy movie?
Could I use the controller to turn the voice up?
How can I call the subtitles out?
What kind of movies do you have?
How can I search a movie?
How can I pause the movie?
Could you please teach me how to fast forward the movie?
Could you please help me to select a comedy?
Sure.
Let me help you.
You can select by your controller.
Here you are.
Push the … button.

7.2.2　Dialogues

(P: Passenger　A: Attendant)

P: Ma'am, what kind of movies do you have on the IFE?
A: We have comedy, romantic, action movies, horror movies and a lot.
P: Do you need some help to select?
A: I can do it myself, thank you.

A: Excuse me, Sir. What can I do for you?
P: Oh, could you please teach me how to use it?
A: Certainly, let me show you the way to use it.
P: OK.
A: For headsets, put the plug into the hole at your armrest. You can choose different channels by pressing those number buttons on the armrest, and then adjust the volume as you wish.
P: Oh, thank you.

（**In Economy Class**）

P: The screen of my seat is not working well.

A: Sorry for the inconvenience, Sir. The on-board entertainment equipment for this seat is not working. So, would you mind changing a seat?

P: OK.

A: Please move to the 35A seat.

P: How can this movie be fast forwarded?

A: Press the fast forward button here.

P: Oh, thank you. I made it.

A: You are welcome.

7.2.3 Cultural Background

Movies Update

Every three months, the related airline department will update the stored videos. Video entertainment is provided via a large video screen at the front of a cabin section, as well as smaller monitors situated every few rows above the aisles. Sound is supplied via the same headphones as those distributed for audio entertainment.

However, personal televisions (PTVs) for every passenger provide passengers with channels broadcasting new and classic films, as well as comedies, news, sports programs, documentaries, children's shows, and drama series. Some airlines also present news and current affairs programs, which are often pre-recorded and delivered in the early morning before flights start off.

PTVs are operated via an In-flight Management System which stores pre-recorded channels on a central server and streams them to PTV equipped seats during flight. AVOD systems store individual programs separately, allowing a passenger to have a specific program streamed to them privately, and be able to control the playback.

Some airlines also provide video games as part of the video entertainment system. For example, passengers on some flights of Singapore Airlines have access to a number of Super Nintendo games as part of its Kris World entertainment system. Also Virgin America's and Virgin Australia's Entertainment System offer passengers internet games over a Linux-based operating system.

7.3 Music

7.3.1 Language Points and Useful Sentence Patterns

7.3.1.1 Language Points

1. Hip-hop

a type of popular dance music with a regular heavy beat and spoken words

2. Rock music

popular music usually played by instruments like guitar and drums and characterized by a persistent heavily accented beat and often country, folk, and blues elements

3. Jazz

a type of music that has a strong beat and parts for performs to play alone

4. Chinese music

Music from China

5. play

the conduct, course, or action of a game

6. pause

a temporary stop

7. fast forward

a function of an electronic device that advances a recording or a video at a higher speed than normal

8. rewind

to wind again

9. volume controller

to control the degree of loudness or the intensity of a sound

10. stop

to close up or block off

7.3.1.2 Useful Sentence Patterns

How can I play the songs?
Which actors do you have in this system?
Do you have a country music album?
Could you help me to plug in the headphones?
Can I search my favorite singer here?
Do you have the Taylor Swift's songs?

7

How can I pause the music?

Which kind of music do you like?

Press the pause key.

Here is the headphone jack.

Can you hear that?

I'm sorry to interrupt you but…

7.3.2　Dialogues

(P: Passenger　A: Attendant)

P: I want to listen to music. What should I do?

A: First you should plug the headphones into the jack.

P: OK, what next?

A: You can select a music type that you like.

P: Oh, now I have it. Thank you.

P: Excuse me, ma'am. I'm old. I don't know how to use this system. Could you help me select a movie?

A: Sure. What type of movie do you want to watch? Romantic, comedy, or action ?

P: Comedy please.

A: We have *Green Collar* and *Zootopia*. Which one do you want?

P: This one will be fine. Thank you.

7.3.3　Cultural Background

In-flight entertainment

In-flight entertainment (IFE) refers to the entertainment available to aircraft passengers during a flight. In 1936, the airship Hindenburg offered passengers a piano, a lounge, a dining room, a smoking room, and a bar during the 2.5 day flight between Europe and America. After the Second World War, IFE was delivered in the form of food and drink services, along with an occasional projector movie during lengthy flights. In 1985 the first personal audio player was offered to passengers, along with noise cancelling headphones in 1989.During the 1990s, the demand for better IFE was a major factor in the design of aircraft cabins. Before then, passengers could expect it was no more than a movie project at the front of a cabin, which could be heard via a headphone at his or her seat. Now, in most aircraft, private IFE TV screens are provided.

Design issues for IFE include system safety, cost efficiency, software reliability, hardware maintenance, and user compatibility.

The in-flight entertainment are frequently managed by content service providers.

The companies involved are in a constant battle to cut costs of production, without lowering the system's quality and compatibility. Cutting production costs may be achieved by anything from altering the housing for personal televisions, to reduce the amount of embedded software in the in-flight entertainment processor. Difficulties with cost are also present with the customers, or airlines, looking to purchase in-flight entertainment systems. Most in-flight entertainment systems are purchased by existing airlines as an upgrade package to an existing fleet of aircraft. This cost can be anywhere from $2 million to $5 million for a plane to be equipped with a set of seat back LCD monitors and an embedded IFE system. Some of the IFE systems are being purchased already installed in a new aircraft, such as the Airbus A320.

7.4　Games

7.4.1　Language Points and Useful Sentence Patterns

7.4.1.1　Language Points

1. electronic

of or relating to electrons

2. involve

to engage as a participant

3. interaction

mutual or reciprocal action or influence

4. dimensional

measure in one direction

5. feedback

the transmission of evaluative or corrective information about an action, event, or process to the original or controlling source

6. platform

a device or structure incorporating or providing a platform

7. arcade

a long arched building or gallery

8. affordable

able to be afforded : having a cost that is not too high

9. console

an architectural member projecting from a wall to form a bracket or from a keystone for ornament

10. purpose

something set up as an object or end to be attained

7.4.1.2　Useful Sentence Patterns

What kind of game do you have?

Do you have a racing car game?

How can I control the car?

Which key is the throttle?

How to draft in this game?

You can use the cross key in the controller to play the game.

Could you please help me find a game?

May I show you how to use this entertainment system?

Press the "X" key to pass the ball.

Here is the instruction of this game.

7.4.2　Dialogues

(P: Passenger　A: Attendant)

P: Ma'am, where can I find the game of *Gluttonous Snake*?

A: You can press the next page button.

P: Oh, I'll try.

A: Do you find what you want?

P: Yes, I get it.

P: Is there a Wi-Fi on board?

A: Yes, there is.

P: Could you help me connect the Wi-Fi here?

A: Sure, I will provide you a password and you can click on the Wi-Fi connection, then it will jump to the web page and you can enter the seat number to connect to the internet.

P: Oh, it works. Thank you.

P: Why can't I connect to Wi-Fi?

A: I'm sorry, Sir. The Wi-Fi on board is not free.

P: How should I pay for that?

A: You can use credit cards to pay and then you can use the Wi-Fi. Do you need my help to show you how that?

P: No, I'm good. Thank you.

7.4.3　Cultural Background

Video games

A video game is an electronic game that involves interaction with a user interface to generate visual feedback on a two- or three-dimensional video display device such as a TV screen, virtual reality headset or computer monitor. Since the 1980s, video games have become increasingly important in the entertainment industry, and whether they are also a form of art is a matter of dispute.

The electronic systems used to play video games are called platforms. Video games are developed and released for one or several platforms and may not be available on others. Specialized platforms such as arcade games, which presented the game in a large, typically coin-operated chassis, were common in the 1980s in video arcades, but declined in popularity as more affordable platforms became available. These include dedicated devices such as video game consoles, as well as general-purpose computers like a laptop, desktop or hand-held computing devices.

The input device used for games and the game controller varies across platforms. Common controllers include game pads, joysticks, mouse devices, keyboards, the touchscreens of mobile devices, or even a person's body, using a Kinect sensor. Players view the game on a display device such as a television or computer monitor or sometimes on virtual reality head-mounted display goggles. There are often game sound effects, music and voice actor lines which come from loudspeakers or headphones. Some games in the 2000s include haptic, vibration-creating effects, force feedback peripherals and virtual reality headsets.

In the 2010s, the commercial importance of the video game industry is increasing. The emerging Asian markets and mobile games on smart phones in particular are driving the growth of the industry. As of 2018, video games generated sales of US$134.9 billion annually worldwide, and were the third-largest segment in the U.S. entertainment market, behind broadcast and cable TV.

7.5 Flight Parameters

7.5.1 Language Points and Useful Sentence Patterns

7.5.1.1 Language Points

1. attitude

the opinions and feelings that you usually have about something

2. altitude

the vertical elevation of an object above the sea

3. speed

the rate at which something moves or travels

4. position

the place where someone or something is

5. heading

something that forms or serves as a head

6. oriental

relating to, or situated in the orient

7. ETA

estimated time of arrival

8. knot

a division of the log's line serving to measure a ship's speed

9. Mach

a usually high speed expressed by a Mach number

10. temperature

degree of hotness or coldness measured on a definite scale

7.5.1.2 Useful Sentence Patterns

How long do we have to fly to destination?

When can we get to New York?

What type of aircraft are we sitting on now?

The map will show our present position.

The plane on this screen indicates our status.

This indicator shows the airplane heading.

The system shows us the information and status of the airplane.

You can ask me any time.

7.5.2　Dialogues

(P: Passenger　A: Attendant)

P: Hi, when is our ETA?

A: It's 20:00 London time.

P: Alright, what's the temperature over there?

A: It's 22 degrees Celsius.

P: Alright, thanks.

P: Hi, how high are we now?

A: Sir, it's around 10400m.

P: WOW, that's so high.

A: Indeed, Sir, but it's still comfortable inside the cabin. It's a good plane.

P: Yes, I'll take your flight again next time.

P: Hi, what's the weather like in London? I'd like to know what kind of clothes I should wear.

A: It's a sunny day at 25 degrees Celsius. I think the T-shirt you are in is perfect.

P: That's a lovely day. Thank you sweetheart.

7.5.3 Cultural Background

A moving-map system

A moving-map system is a real-time flight information video channel broadcast through cabin project/video screens and personal televisions (PTVs). In addition to displaying a map that illustrates the position and direction of the plane, the system gives the altitude, airspeed, outside air temperature, distance to the destination, distance from the origination point, and local time. The moving-map system information is derived in real time from the aircraft's flight computer systems.

The first moving-map system designed for passengers was named Airshow and introduced in 1982. It was invented by Airshow Inc (ASINC), a small southern California corporation, which later became part of Rockwell Collins. KLM and Swissair were the first airlines to offer the moving map systems to their passengers.

The latest versions of moving-maps offered by IFE manufacturers include Adonis One IFE, ICARUS Moving Map Systems, Airshow 4200 by Rockwell Collins, iXlor2 by Panasonic Avionics and Jet Map HD by Honeywell Aerospace. In 2013, Betria Interactive unveiled FlightPath3D, a fully interactive moving-map that enables passengers to zoom and pan around a 3D world map using touch gestures, similar to Google Earth. FlightPath3D was chosen by Norwegian as the moving-map on their new fleet of Boeing 787 Dreamliners, running on Panasonic's Android based touch-screen IFE system.

After the attempted Christmas Day bombing of 2009, the United States Transportation Security Administration (TSA) briefly ordered the live-map shut-off on international flights landing in the United States. Some airlines complained that doing so may compel the entire IFE system to remain shut. After complaints from airlines and passengers alike, these restrictions were eased.

7.6 Business and First Class

7.6.1 Language Points and Useful Sentence Patterns

7.6.1.1 Language Points

1. passenger safety

the safety of on board passengers

2. **captain**

the pilot in command of a civil aircraft

3. **pre-flight safety demonstration**

a safety demonstration before a plane takes off on safety procedures in the event of an emergency

4. **emergency exits**

a special exit only used during an emergency

5. **seat belt**

a belt or strap securing a person to prevent injury, esp. ecially in a vehicle or aircraft

6. **lavatory**

toilet

7. **armrest**

a padded or upholstered arm of a chair or other seat on which a sitter's arm can comfortably rest

8. **reading light**

a personal light you can turn on when main lights on the aircraft are off.

9. **overhead luggage compartment**

a storage container usually above passenger seats in a plane.

7.6.1.2 Useful Sentence Patterns

Welcome aboard.
Here are your slippers.
What do you want to drink?
Do you need a blanket?
When will you want to have a meal, Sir?
What kind of wine do you like?
Today's appetizer is …
Let me help you to take the tray away.
May I help you close the window shad?

7.6.2 Dialogues

(A: Attendant   P: Passenger)

A: Excuse me, Sir. Would you like me to introduce you how to use the in-flight entertainment system?

P: Yes, please.

A: This is our portable multimedia device designed exclusively for our distinguished passengers in the first class. Would you like me to turn it on?

P: Yes, please.

A: There are a variety of programs for you to choose from and enjoy.

P: Sounds good.

A: Click ENTER key and select the language, then you will see the HOME page. On this page, there are 7 channels. They're MOVIE, TV, MUSIC, GAMES, CHILDREN and ex-connect.

P: That's wonderful. Thank you.

A: Do you want to watch movies or listen to music now?

P: I would like to listen to the classical music now.

A: Sure. You can make your selections from the programs.

P: Thank you.

A: You are welcome. It is my pleasure. Press the call button whenever you need any help, please.

7.6.3 Cultural Background

The First-class cabin

First-class seats vary from large reclining seats with more legroom and width than other classes to suites with a fully reclining seat, workstation and TV surrounded by privacy dividers. International first-class seats usually have 147–239 cm of seat pitch and 48–89 cm of width while domestic flights may have 86–173 cm of pitch and 46–56 cm in width. In fact, this means it is less discomfort for taller people. Some airlines have first-class seats which allow one guest sit for a short while face-to-face with the occupant of the cabin.

First-class passengers usually have at least one or more than one on larger planes, lavatory for their exclusive use. Business- and economy-class passengers are not normally permitted in the first-class cabin. Normally AVOD (audiovisual on demand) entertainment is offered, although sometimes normal films, television programs and interactive games are provided on medium-large seat-back or armrest-mounted flat panel monitors. Especially for long-haul and high-yielding routes on top airlines, a first-class seat may have facilities akin to a five-star hotel, such as a mini-bar.

Since the 1990s, a trend has developed in which many airlines eliminated first class sections in favor of an upgraded business class. Newer business class seating is increasing adding features which are previously exclusive to first class such as convertible lie-flat seats, narrowing the amenities gap to an extent that first class is redundant. Furthermore, with the late 2000s recession, airlines have removed or not installed first class seating in their aircraft, as first class seats are usually double the price of business class but can take up more than twice the room, leaving business class the most expensive seats on such planes. However some, such as Garda Indonesia, have opted to reintroduce first class seating sections with new aircraft.

Unit 8
Meal and Drink Service

8.1 Meal Service

8.1.1 Language Points and Useful Sentence Patterns

8.1.1.1 Language Points

1. routine

a regular course of procedure; habitual or mechanical performance of an established procedure

2. meal

an act or the time of eating a portion of food to satisfy appetite; the portion of food eaten at a meal

3. service

the occupation or function of serving

4. Muslim meal

The food for Muslim

5. Vegetarian

a person who does not eat meat or fish: someone whose diet consists wholly of vegetables, fruits, grains, nuts, and sometimes eggs or dairy products

6. Kosher meal

The food for Kosher

7. fast food

Relating to, or specializing in food that can be prepared and served quickly

8. refreshments

something (such as food or drink) that refreshes

9. provide

to supply or make available (something wanted or needed)

10. main tray

an open receptacle with a flat bottom and a low rim for holding, carrying, or exhibiting articles

8.1.1.2 Useful Sentence Patterns

Do you need to add some water, Sir?

What do you want for the appetizer?

Here is the knife and fork.

May I have some napkins?

Unit 8 Meal and Drink Service

What kind of beverage do you want?
Do you need to add some ice inside?
Could you please straighten the seat back?
Let me take it.
Could you hand me the cup?

8.1.2 Dialogues

(A: Attendant   P: Passenger   PS: Purser)

A: We have meat and seafood today. Which one would you prefer?
P: Meat, please.
A: Certainly. / Here you are.

(AFTER THE MEAL)

A: Have you finished your meal?
P: Yes.
A: I'll take it away.
P: Thank you.
PS: The passenger on 2A is a CIP passenger.
A: What is the difference among the VIP, VVIP and CIP?
PS: VIP passengers are divided into special VIP, or general important passenger.
A: What should I do for him?
PS: Before the VIP passenger boarding the flight, the online business information of the flight will show the required meal of the VIP, and the meal center could provide the passenger a VIP-specific meal and meal standard.
A: What kind of passengers could be provided with the menu?
PS: Only the business class passengers, first class passengers and VIP passengers could have a menu of meals.
A: Okay.
PS: By the way, for special needs of passengers, such as wheelchair passengers, stretcher passengers, unaccompanied elderly or children, they should be properly handed over to the company's ground service personnel after registration.

8.1.3 Cultural Background

Star Alliance

Star Alliance is one of the world's largest global airline alliances which founded on May 14 in 1997. Its current CEO is Jeffrey Goth and its headquarters are located in Frankfurt am Main, Germany. As of April 2018, Star Alliance has been the second largest global alliance by

19

passenger count with 728 million, behind Sky Team and ahead of One World. Its slogan is "The Way the Earth Connects".

Star Alliance's 28 member airlines operate a fleet of approximately 4,657 aircrafts, serving more than 1330 airports in 192 countries on more than 18500 daily departures. The alliance has a two-tier rewards program, Silver and Gold, with incentives including priority boarding and upgrades. Like other airline alliances, Star Alliance airlines share airport terminals and many member planes are painted in the alliance's livery.

On 14 May 1997, an agreement was announced forming Star Alliance from five airlines on three continents: United Airlines, Scandinavian Airlines, Thai Airways, Air Canada, and Lufthansa. The alliance chose Young & Rubicon for advertising, with a budget of $25 million. The airlines shared the star logo from the beginning, with its five points representing the founding airlines. The alliance adopted its first slogan, "The Airline Network for Earth", with its goal "an alliance that will take passengers to every major city on earth".

The now defunct Brazilian airline VARIG joined the Star Alliance network on 22 October 1997, extending the alliance into South America. Also joining were a set Australia and Air New Zealand, expanding Star Alliance to Australia and the Pacific. With the addition of the latter two carriers, the alliance served 720 destinations in 110 countries with a combined fleet of 1650 aircraft. The next airline to join was All Nippon Airways (ANA), the group's second Asian airline, on 15 October 1999.

8.2　Drinks Service

8.2.1　Language Points and Useful Sentence Patterns

8.2.1.1　Language Points

1. beverage

   a drinkable liquid

2. Assort

   to distribute into groups of a like kind : CLASSIFY

3. variety

   the quality or state of having different forms or types : MULTIFARIOUSNESS

4. cater

   to provide a supply of food

5. spirit

   an animating or vital principle held to give life to physical organisms

6. crucial

important, significant

7. myriad

ten thousand

8. emphasis

force or intensity of expression that gives impressiveness or importance to something

8.2.1.2 Useful Sentence Patterns

May I help you fill some coffee?

Could you introduce what kind of wine you have?

What about Champagne?

Enjoy it.

Wonderful!

Couldn't be better.

It tastes good.

May I try a little?

How does it taste like?

8.2.2 Dialogues

(A: Attendant   P: Passenger   PS: Purser)

A: Would you like something to drink?

(1)

P: Orange juice, please.

A: Certainly. Here you are.

(2)

P: Wine, please.

A: Yes. We have red (wine) and white (wine).

Which would you prefer?

P: Red (wine), please.

A: Certainly, here you are.

(3)

P: What do you have?

A: We have beer, whisky, fruit juice and other drinks.

P: Whisky, please.

A: Certainly.

(TO THE NEXT PAX)

A: Ma'am/Sir, what would you like?

P: Beer, please.

A: OK. We have Tsingtao, Harbin, Budweiser and others.

P: Tsingtao, please.

A: Certainly.

(ITEM NOT AVAILABLE)

A: Would you like something to drink?

P: Iced coffee, please.

A: I'm sorry / I'm afraid, we don't have iced coffee. Would you like some other drinks?

P: Orange juice, then.

A: Certainly.

A: Would you like another drink (second helping)?

P: No, thank you.

A: I see, ma'am/Sir.

(REFILL)

A: What details do I need to pay attention to, while I am providing the drink service?

PS: We should present and pour wine and champagne to our passengers in the aisle, present the bottle by holding the bottle by the lower portion with the label.

A: How should I hold the bottle when I serve?

PS: Do not touch the bottle to the rim of glass.

A: I got it, what other manners should I do?

PS: We always offer the passengers small taste of wine, fulfill the glass about 2/3 full. Twist bottle away to ensure that it doesn't drip. And always hold high ball glasses by the stem.

A: Okay.

A: If I serve the Champagne, what manners do we have?

PS: First, we place linen over the cork and wire seal. With the bottle facing away from people, release the wire seal and cork, twist the wire seal and then pour in two steps, fill 1/3 of the glass and allow the bubbles to settle, and then complete pouring until the glass is 2/3 full.

A: I got it.

8.2.3　Cultural Background

In-flight Service

Typical in-flight service aboard a general aviation aircraft begins with a snack and beverage presentation. Depending on the time of day, various beverage options-ranging from juices, coffees, and teas to assorted varieties of alcohol-may be considered. Within these categories are wide ranges of possibilities. There are numerous options and variations in tea and coffee services for example. The goal, in any beverage service, is to enhance the passenger flight experience.

In-flight caterers can be an invaluable resource in terms of beverage and food pairings-especially in the realm of wine selection. Spirits are generally similar worldwide and not as crucial to the food service as they're served separately from main courses. Wines, however, tend to be more local in nature and are consumed in many cases with entrees. The right wine and beverage selections will significantly elevate the entire passenger flight experience. Don't let the beverage service be an afterthought.

There is a myriad of garnish options available for in-flight beverages. These range from citrus slices to salt and various herbs. Instead of using regular salt, consider a smoked or black salt (a pure salt from the Hawaiian Islands mixed with charcoal to help digestion). If you're serving Nouvelle cuisine, be sure that beverages and beverage garnishes match entree presentations. Nouvelle cuisine is characterized by lighter, more delicate dishes, with a greater emphasis on presentation. You'll also want to consider health and religious restrictions and whether or not your passengers consume alcohol. Non-alcoholic beverage options might include a minted melon juice, watermelon with black pepper, or a smoothie with Greek yogurt.

8.3 Children and Senior People

8.3.1 Language Points and Useful Sentence Patterns

8.3.1.1 Language Points

1. BBML

suitable for meals for babies under 2 years of age.

2. CHML

suitable for children from two to twelve years of age.

3. HNML

A non-vegetarian meal made according to the religious beliefs and eating habits of Indians.

4. KSML

Purchased from manufacturers with Jewish meal production qualifications and credit certification, making meals and providing services according to Jewish religious laws and eating habits.

5. MOML

A meal made with a Muslim meal production qualification, based on Muslim religious laws and eating habits.

6. VJML

Indian vegetarian food prepared.

7. NBML

Does not include meals of beef, veal or related products.

8. BLML

The meal is soft, low in fat, low in fiber and free of irritating ingredients.

9. DBML

A meal suitable for diabetics that does not contain any kind of sugar.

10. LCML

Limit the amount of fat, seasonings, gravy and fried ingredients; limit sugary ingredients.

8.3.1.2 Useful Sentence Patterns

What kind of meal do you want?

May I ask for a CHML?

How can I order the KSML?

Do you have a meal for children?

May I be of any assistance?

Would you like something to …

8.3.2　Dialogues

(P: Passenger　A: Attendant)

P: Hi, do you have low cholesterol meal?

A: Yes, Sir. We do have, when do you want to have?

P: As soon as you are ready.

A: Sure, won't be long, enjoy your flight, Sir.

(After the meal)

P: By the way, do you have any sparkling water?

A: Yes, Sir. We do have. Do you want iced sparkling water?

P: That would be wonderful! I want 2 bottles, please.

A: No problem, Sir.

P: Thank you so much.

8.3.3　Cultural Background

Sky Team

Sky Team is an airline alliance. Founded in June 2000, Sky Team was the last of the three major airline alliances to be formed, the first two being Star Alliance and One world. Its annual passenger count is 730 million, the largest of the three major alliances. As of January 2019, Sky Team consisted of 19 carriers from five continents and operated with the slogan "Caring more about you". It also operates a cargo alliance named Sky Team Cargo, which partners ten carriers, and all of them are Sky Team members. Its centralized management team, Sky Team Central, is based at the World Trade Center Schiphol Airport on the grounds of Amsterdam Airport Schiphol in Amsterdam, Netherlands.

In 2004, the alliance had its biggest expansion when Continental Airlines, Northwest Airlines and KLM simultaneously joined as full members. In 2010, the alliance celebrated its 10th anniversary with the introduction of a special livery, the joining or upgrading status of four airlines, followed by the announcements of Aerolineas Argentinas, China Airlines, and Garuda Indonesia to become full members. In January 2011, incorporated with both Saudi Arabian Airlines and Middle East Airlines during 2012; these events effectively took place in May and June 2012, respectively, whereas Aerolineas Argentinas and Xiamen Airlines memberships were activated in August and November in the same year, respectively. Garuda Indonesia entered the alliance in March 2014.

As of November 2018, Sky Team flies to more than 1000 destinations in more than 170 countries and operates more than 17000 daily flights. The alliance and its members have 750 lounges worldwide.

8.4 Cockpit Catering

8.4.1 Language Points and Useful Sentence Patterns

8.4.1.1 Language Points

1. simple

free from guile

2. snack

a light meal: food eaten between regular meals

3. haul

to cause (something) to move by pulling or drawing : to exert traction on

4. incorporate

to unite or work into something already existent so as to form an indistinguishable whole

5. element

any of the four substances air, water, fire, and earth formerly believed to compose the physical universe

6. cuisine

manner of preparing food : style of cooking

7. primary

first in order of time or development

8. domestic

living near or about human habitations

9. multiple

consisting of, including, or involving more than one

10. reflective

capable of reflecting light, images, or sound waves

8.4.1.2 Useful Sentence Patterns

Would you mind my waking you up when I sever the meal?
Would you like adding some water?
What can I do for you?
When should I enter the cockpit?
Could you please help me fill my water bottle?
Could you do me a favor?

8.4.2 Dialogues

(A: Attendant   CA: Captain   P: Passerger)

A：Captain, when will you want to eat the meal today?

CA: You can serve 30 minutes later, after the 10000ft.

A: No problem, so which kind of meal would you want today?

CA: Healthy meal.

A: OK, see you later.

A: Would you like something to drink? Tea or coffee?

P: Iced water, please, if you have got.

A: I'm sorry/ I'm afraid we don't have iced water. What about some other cold drinks, like orange juice or apple juice?

P: Apple juice, then.

A: All right, here you are.

8.4.3 Cultural Background

Airline meals

An airline meal, airline food, or in-flight meal is a meal served to passengers on board a commercial airliner. These meals are prepared by special airline catering services and normally served to passengers using an airline service trolley.

These meals vary widely in quality and quantity across different airline companies and classes of travel. They range from a simple snack or beverage in short-haul economy class to a seven-course gourmet meal in a first class long-haul flight. The types of food offered also vary widely from country to country, and often incorporate elements of local cuisine, sometimes both from the origin and destination countries. When ticket prices were regulated in the American domestic market, food was the primary means airlines differentiated themselves.

The first airline meals were served by Handley Page Transport, an airline company founded in 1919, to serve the London–Paris route in October of that year. Passengers could choose from a selection of sandwiches and fruit.

The type of food varies depending upon the Airline Company and class of travel. Meals may be served on one tray or in multiple courses with no tray and with a tablecloth, metal cutlery, and glassware. Often the food is reflective of the culture of the country the airline is based in or the country that the airplane is destined for (e.g. Indian, Japanese, Chinese, or Western meals).

The airline dinner typically includes meat, fish, or pasta; a salad or vegetable; a small bread roll; and a dessert. Condiments are supplied in small sachets or shakers.

Caterers usually produce alternative meals for passengers with restrictive diets. These must usually be ordered at least 24 hours in advance, sometimes when buying the ticket.

8.5   Customs of Different Countries

8.5.1   Language Points and Useful Sentence Patterns

8.5.1.1   Language Points

1. predominant

having superior strength, influence, or authority: prevailing

2. dietary

the kinds and amounts of food available to or eaten by an individual, group, or population

3. consume

to do away with completely: destroy

4. ingredient

something that enters into a compound or is a component part of any combination or mixture

5. liberate

to set at liberty: free

6. taboo

banned on grounds of morality or taste

7. bravery

the quality or state of having or showing mental or moral strength to face danger, fear, or difficulty : the quality or state of being brave

8. courage

mental or moral strength to venture, persevere, and withstand danger, fear, or difficulty

9. vase

a usually round vessel of greater depth than width used chiefly as an ornament or for holding flowers

10. marriage

the state of being united as spouses in a consensual and contractual relationship recognized by law

8.5.1.2 Useful Sentence Patterns

Make sure that...
Never do...
It's considered...
You are expected to...
The announcements are also transmitted to...
The committee comprises five persons.
The cabin attendants will do their best to serve the passengers.

8.5.2 Dialogues

(A: Attendant   PS: Purser)

A: The passenger on 12F seat ordered a Muslim meal, so what's its difference on it?

PS: Muslim meal is a meal with a Muslim meal production qualification, based on the Muslim religious laws and eating habits. There is no pork inside. Normally is mutton beef or chicken.

A: What other special meals do we have?

PS: Kosher meal is purchased from a manufacturer with Jewish meal production qualification and reputation, making meals and providing services according to Jewish religious laws and dining habits. And all the food needs to show to passengers before giving them, and ask them whether they need flight attendants to help them to cook. If they want to heat by themselves, we have a special oven for them in the galley.

A: Oh, what about the meal for babies?

PS: Baby meal is suitable for babies under two years of age. Normally is puree, vegetable puree, mashed potatoes and etc.

8.5.3 Cultural Background

Customs of Different Countries

Teeth tossing in Greece: Some cultures will pop children's teeth under their pillows and wait for a swap with cold hard cash by a fairy. Others throw a baby's recently liberated tooth on their roofs.

Baby jumping in Spain: Residents in a small Northern Community take part in baby jumping called El Colacho, to keep the devil at bay. Men dressed as the devil run between and jump over infants, who are laid on mattresses along the streets.

Avoiding using red ink in South Korea: Based on their history and customs, red ink is used to write down names of dead people. It is therefore considered a taboo to write someone's name in red.

Initiation custom in Brazil: It is strange how young boys prove their bravery and strength. In the Satare Mawe tribe they showcase the courage by placing hands in a basket filled with angry bullet ants. The bites are real pain.

The Monkey Buffet Festival in Thailand: Some people might be surprised to be looking at some monkeys atop a buffet table, feasting on sumptuous dishes. In this annual festivity, over 3000 kg of fruits and vegetables are fed to several monkeys that dwell in Lopburi, Bangkok.

Tomato craze in Spain: La Tomatina is the biggest tomato fight that exists. It is a strange culture among the Valencians in Bunol where tomatoes are used as weapons. Snowball fights are so last year.

The Polterabend custom in Germany: Just before couples are wed, their families and close friends meet for an informal affair. Then, all guests are requested to break things such as dinner wares and flower vases, anything except glasses. As soon as the entire place is in disarray, the couples should clear up the broken things. This tradition shows the couple the significance of being united and of hard work, which is necessary to make their marriage works. At least they are in for a hell of a start. Things can only improve from here.

8.6 Dining Etiquette

8.6.1 Language Points and Useful Sentence Patterns

8.6.1.1 Language Points

1. casual

subject to, resulting from, or occurring by chance

2. acceptable

capable or worthy of being accepted

3. elbow

the joint of the human arm

4. interfere

to interpose in a way that hinders or impedes: come into collision or be in opposition

5. region

an administrative area, division, or district

6. attention

the act or state of applying the mind to something

7. host

one that receives or entertains guests socially, commercially, or officially

8. etiquette

formal rules for polite behaviour in society or in a particular group

9. professional

of, relating to, or characteristic of a profession

10. respond

to do something as a reaction to something that has been said or done

8.6.1.2　Useful sentence patterns

It is indisputable that…

It is commonly believed that…

There is no doubt that…

I can't say…

If it hadn't been for…

What's the matter with…?

What's your favorite…?

We may as well…

The first thing I'm going to do when… is…

It is widely acknowledged that…

8.6.2　Dialogues

(A: Attendant　PS: Purser　P: Passenger)

A: Purser, what's the difference between eastern style meal and western style meal?

PS: Eastern style food is generally rice and formal dishes; we have different cuisines such as Cantonese cuisine, Sichuan cuisine, and etc. Western food is mainly spaghetti, pasta, burger, cakes,etc.

A: So what kind of meals do we have on board?

PS: We have both styles of food on board, so that the passengers can choose thei meal according to their personal preferences.

    A: Here is your hot towel.

    P: Thanks.

    A: Something to drink?

    P: Wine, please.

    A: We have red wine and white wine. Which one would you prefer?

    P: Red, please.

    A: Certainly. Here you are.

    P: Hi, I want some drinks. What do you have?

    A: We have beer, whisky, fruit juice and some other drinks. What do you like?

    P: Whisky, please.

    A: Okay.

(TO THE NEXT PASSENGER)

    A: What would you like?

    P: Beer, please.

    A: OK. We have Kirin, Asahi, Sapporo and some others.

    P: Kirin, please.

    A: Certainly.

8.6.3 Cultural Background

Table manners

Although dining out has become more casual, it still isn't acceptable to talk with your mouth full of food, rock the table with your elbows, or interfere with other diners' experiences by displaying improper etiquette. It's important to follow certain manners guidelines in both formal settings and fast food restaurants.

Table manners are important in both professional and social situations, so it's a good idea to know some basics. There may be some slight variations, depending on your region and what is locally acceptable. So if you are at a dinner party, pay attention to the host or hostess and take cues from them.

Here are some tips to show that you know how to behave at the table.

Using proper etiquette at the table will also help you socially and professionally in a restaurant or in someone's home.

Before the dinner. If you are invited to have dinner with someone, it is always a good idea to respond, even if an RSVP is not requested. This helps with planning. Don't ask if you can bring extra guests if the invitation doesn't make the offer. However, if your family is invited to someone's home for dinner, it is okay to ask if your children are included. If they are, make sure your children know good manners before they go.

When to eat. If you are eating out, you should wait until all the members of your group have been served before picking up your fork. At a private dinner, observe the host or hostess and pick up your fork when he or she does. However, if you are at a buffet, you may start when there are others seated at your table.

After you finish eating, partially fold your napkin and place it to the left of your plate. Wait until the host or hostess signals that the meal is over, you may stand. After the meal, don't eat and run. If nothing is planned after dinner, stick around for approximately an hour before saying good-bye to the host and thanking him or her for the dinner. If the event are informal, you may offer to help clean up.

Unit 9
Duty-free Sales

9.1 Enquiring In-flight Duty-free Sales

9.1.1 Language Points and Useful Sentence Patterns

9.1.1.1 Language Points

1. duty-free

refers to an amount received or paid that is not subject to taxation

2. catalog

a book or pamphlet containing an enumeration of things

3. currency

the metal or paper medium of exchange that is presently used

4. jewelry

an adornment (as a bracelet or ring or necklace) made of precious metals and set with gems (or imitation gems)

5. perfume

a toiletry that emits and diffuses a fragrant odor

6. alcoholic drink

a liquor or brew containing alcohol as the active agent

9.1.1.2 Useful Sentence Patterns

1. Express advice or suggestion

How about... ?

What about... ?

Why don't you ... ?

You'd better (not)...

It's a good idea to do ...

2. Express willingness and unwillingness

willingness

I'm glad to ...

I'm willing to do ...

I would like ...

I would rather do ...

I prefer to ...

unwillingness

I don't really want to ...

I don't really fancy doing ...

I wouldn't be willing to do ...

I'm afraid I can't possibly do ...

9.1.2　Dialogues

Setting: It's 16:00 on Wednesday (local time). Passengers are boarding Air China Flight CA887 from Beijing to Los Angeles. The flight attendants are going to offer in-flight duty-free service.

(A: Attendant　P: Passenger)

P: Excuse me, Miss. Could you come over for help, please?

A: Sure, what can I help you?

P: I'd like to buy some gifts for my friends in Los Angeles.

A: What would you like to buy, Sir?

P: I have no idea. What kinds of products dose this flight offer?

A: Do you mind telling me something about your friends?

P: Of course not. They are couples and my business partners. This is my first time to visit them.

A: Well, we offer a wide range of products, which includes over 80 items from the world's most popular brands: jewelry from Swarovski, Pandora, Tiffany, watches from SEIKO, TISSOT, LONGINES, sunglasses from GUCCI, RayBan, Prada, perfume from Burberry, Chanel, Dior, Lancome, Versace. We also have alcoholic drink, such as Remy Martin, Johnnie Walker Red Label and Black Label, Chivas Regal, Jack Daniels.

P: The exclusive collection on this flight is really impressive. Please let me think about it. By the way, how do I get to pay?

A: We accept cash, credit cards and cheque. How are you willing to pay?

P: I'd like to pay by credit cards.

A: Sure, Sir. We accept all the major credit cards, such as Visa, MasterCard and American Express.

P: Great. I'll let you know when I'm ready to order.

A: No problem, Sir. Enjoy your shopping.

P: Thank you very much.

A: You're welcome.

Setting: After the in-flight shopping announcement, there is a passenger pressing the call button.

(A: Attendant　P: Passenger)

A: Hello, madam. Did you press the call button? Is there anything I can assist with?

P: Yes, it's me. I just heard the announcement that duty-free shopping is available on board. The price sounds attractive. I'd like to buy some gifts for my family members. But I didn't find the collection catalog mentioned in the announcement.

A: The catalog is in the seat pocket in front of you. Let me find it for you.

(The attendant checked the pocket, but there wasn't any cope in it.)

A: Sorry, madam. I'll bring a new copy for you right now.

P: It will be appreciated.

A: I'll be back soon.

Setting: While a flight attendant is rolling a trolley in the cabin, a passenger stops her.

A: What can I do for you, Sir?

P: I'd like to buy some alcoholic drink for my friends. Could you give me some ideas?

A: Sure, do you prefer red wine or whisky? We offer high quality France red wine and premium whisky from Chives Regal and Remy Martin.

P: How much does this France red wine cost?

A: It's U.S. $45.

P: Is there any discount if I buy two bottles?

A: Sorry, Sir. All items on board are sold at priced tag.

P: Okay, may I have two bottles, please? What currencies are accepted?

A: No problem, Sir. We accept major currencies, U.S. dollars, Euro and pound sterling.

P: Here you are, $100.

A: Excellent, here are your $10 change and your two bottles of red wine. Hope you enjoy your flight.

P: Thank you so much.

A: It's my pleasure.

9.1.3　Cultural Background

Duty-Free

Duty-free refers to the act of being able to purchase an item in particular circumstances without paying import, sales, value-added or other taxes. Duty-free stores are an enticing perk of international travel. These retail businesses sell merchandise which is exempt from duties and taxes with the understanding they will be taken out of the country for use.

Under ordinary circumstances, host countries expect you to pay an import, sales, value-added (VAT), or local tax on goods you buy. However, when shopping in international airports, sea terminals, onboard cruise ships, and during international airline flights, your purchase is made in no man's land. Hence, you are neither in nor out of any particular host country, including the one in which the terminal is located. No man's land status is a justification for shielding you, as a passenger in transit, from host country taxes.

Duty-free shopping has a twist in the European Union (EU). Goods you buy while traveling between EU countries are duty-paid, or taxable. Products you buy while traveling to, or away from, an EU country is duty-refund, meaning the traveler must apply for a refund of EU's value-added tax.

Duty-free shops sell premium branded high markup luxury goods. Advertisements that duty-free prices are 10% to 50% lower than domestic prices. Due to requirements to use the product outside of the host country, the duty-free shop will package your purchase and deliver it to you as you board for departure.

Merchandise that is duty-free in the host country may be taxed as you return to your home country. Duty-free regulations vary depending on your country of residence, travel destination, and your length of stay. Other rules apply to the items purchased, the cost of the article, and the country of its manufacture.

In the U.S., you will be asked to fill out a U.S. Customs Form to declare any purchases made abroad. Receipts are crucial, as they prove how much was paid for the product. You will owe duties, or tax, on them if their value exceeds the duty-free exemption for the country from which you are returning.

Personal exemptions range between $200 and $1600. Additional regulations include limits on the length of travel abroad and waiting periods between frequent trips. Some items, like alcohol and cigarettes, are limited by the quantity, depending on the country where it was bought. Your allowance for duty-free alcohol from the EU, for example, is one liter. Also, travelers should understand that some products sold in other nations are illegal in the U.S.

9.2 Buying a present

9.2.1 Language Points and Useful Sentence Patterns

9.2.1.1 Language Points

1. credit card

a card (usually plastic) that you use to buy goods or services and pay for them later

2. check

a printed piece of paper that you written an amount of money on and use instead of money pay for things

3. receipt

a written statement shows that you have paid money for something

4. pin number

a number you choose and use to gain access to various accounts

5. budget

a plan of how to spend money

9.2.1.2　Useful Sentence Patterns

1. Expressing agreement and disagreement

agreement

I agree with you.

I'm with you.

I absolutely agree on it.

Good idea.

It sounds good/awesome/great/perfect/fantastic.

disagleemeet

I don't agree with you.

We don't agree on this point.

I'm afraid I can't agree with you.

Not really/exactly.

That's not a good idea.

That sounds terrible/bad/ridiculous.

2. Inquiring for price

How much is it?

What's the price (of it)?

How much money is it?

How much / What does it cost?

9.2.2　Dialogues

(P: passenger　A: attendant)

Setting: While cabin attendants are offering in-flight duty-free service in the cabin, a couple are talking about buying a gift for their son.

Wife: Babe, our trip was so stressful that we didn't have time to buy gifts for our son. What do you think we choose something on the plane for him?

Husband: That's a good idea. (He is looking at the products in the catalog.)

A: Is there anything I can help here, Sir?

Wife: Oh, I'd like to choose something special for your son.

A: How old is your son?

Wife: He's eight years old.

A: For boys, we have toy cars and Lego toys which are customized for our airline.

Husband: It sounds very special. Honey, how do you think about it?

Wife: I think so, too. Could you show us the toys?

A: Certainly, Madam. Wait for a moment, please.

(The cabin attendant returned to the rear cabin to get the toys.)

A: Here are the toys, Madam. We currently have limited edition toys of three scenes: terminals, airplane cabins and aprons. They are very collectible.

Husband: Which one do you think our son would like?

Wife: I think he'll love the apron. Miss, can we have this apron scene, please? How much is it?

P: It's US $ 75.00.

Wife: Okay, I'll have this. Do you take credit cards?

P: Sure, Madam. We accept all the major credit cards.

Wife: Here is my card.

A: Thank you, Madam. It's US $75. Your pin number, please.

Wife: Sure.

A: Could you sign here, please?

Wife: Okay.

A: Thank you. Here's your credit card and the receipt. And take your toy, please.

Husband and Wife: Thank you very much.

A: You're welcome.

P: Excuse me, Miss. Could you come over for help?

A: Yes, Sir. What can I do for you?

P: I want to buy a gift for my mother. But I'm not good at choosing gifts for women. Do you have any suggestion for me?

A: What kind of gift do you want to choose?

P: I just want to choose something more special and practical.

A: What about jewelry? Many ladies like jewelry.

P: Is there something special?

A: I think you asked the right person. We have the bracelet of Pandora's birthday stones series which is only available on our flights.

P: That sounds perfect.

A: What is your mother's birthday month?

P: It's in November.

A: Okay, I'll bring the November birthday stone for you.

P: How much is that?

39

A: It's US $190.00.

P: Great. Here's $200.

A: Thank you, Sir. 190 dollars out of two hundred. Here is your change, 10 dollars. And your bracelet and receipt, please.

P: Thank you for your help.

A: You're welcome.

Setting: a young lady is looking for something in the cart.

A: Hello, Miss. Did you see anything to buy?

P: I'd like to find a gift for my female friend.

A: We have a fabulous collection of gift packs. Would you mind telling me your budget?

P: Well, something within US $100 is fine.

A: We have some gift packs of perfume, mascara and lipstick. They're all at duty-free prices.

P: The lipstick looks nice. How much is one pack?

A: This two-lipsticks pack from Dior is US $100. That three-lipstick pack from MAC is US $89. Buying the gift box is more cost-effective than buying it alone.

P: Good. Can I have that MAC pack, please? I think this pack is perfect.

A: Sure. What does your friend's skin color like?

P: Her skin is a little yellowish.

A: Okay, the color of this orange line is suitable for people with yellow skin.

P: No problem, Miss. Can I have one of these packs, please? You are the best salesman I have ever seen.

A: Thank you for your complements.

P: Can I pay in traveler's checks?

A: Of course.

P: Here you are.

A: Thanks. Here's the lipstick pack you choose. I hope your friend will like it.

P: I think so .Thank you for your professional advice.

A: It's my pleasure.

9.2.3　Cultural Background

Duty-free shopping tips: Buying duty-free goods before getting to the airport
Natalie Paris

Shopping in, airport shops is merely a way of killing time before a flight. Serious shoppers, however, will welcome the news that they can now reserve duty-free products before they arrive at the terminal and find them on their seats when they board the plane.

Passengers flying with Thomas Cook can order anything from a bottle of rum to aftershave up to a month in advance of their flight through its new service, Airshoppen. The airline claims that a range of 1500 products are on offer at prices between 20 and 65 per cent less than those found on the high street. Christoph Debus, chief hotels and airlines officer for Thomas Cook, said: "Airshoppen gives Thomas Cook Airlines' customers the chance to experience that *duty-free shopping* holiday excitement in the comfort of their own home before they've even started packing." He said the service gives customers the opportunity to plan purchases well in advance, avoiding a rush at the airport and ensuring availability. "Their purchases are on their aircraft seat to take on holiday and they can order again for when they come back," he added.

A pre-order duty-free service is offered by some other airlines already. British Airways, for example, offers a pre-order service, or Buy before You Fly, from its High Life shop in November 2013 for most long-haul flights. Orders can be placed three months and up to three days before a customer's flight when ordering online. Home delivery is also available for products such as tobacco, alcohol and some fragrances, which are not applicable due to HM Customs and Excise.

Heathrow Airport also has its own "boutique" service that allows any passengers expecting to fly the chance to first reserve their shopping online, then confirm it up to three days prior to travel, before finally collecting and paying for it at the airport.

World Duty Free, which has branches at Gatwick and Heathrow terminals as well as many others all over the country, has recently introduced an online reservation service also.

Customers can reserve items online and then collect and pay for them in the appropriate airport store from between one month to 24 hours before the departure. Thomas Cook's service is available to all of its customers from December 7, with the first deliveries due on board flights on January 12, 2016. Passengers are told that they can get a refund if they find the products they have reserved available for a cheaper price at the airport.

9.3 Choosing something for oneself

9.3.1 Language Points and Useful Sentence Patterns

9.3.1.1 Language Points

1. brand

a type of product made by a particular company or producer, that has a particular name or design

2. wallet

a pocket-size case for holding and paper money, bank cards etc

3. discount

amount of money taken off the cost of something

4. cost-effective

productive relative to the cost

9.3.1.2 Useful Sentence Patterns

1. Expressing preference

I prefer ... rather than ...

I'd (much)prefer... than...

I like ... better than ...

2. Expressing promise

We keep your promise/word to do ...

I stand by what I said earlier.

I won't let you down.

I'm sure of it.

I swear.

I'm a hundred percent sure.

You can rest assured.

9.3.2 Dialogues

(P: passenger   A: attendant)

P: Excuse me, Miss. I just heard you have many perfume packs on your flight. I'd like to buy some.

A: Yes, we have plenty of packs from nearly all famous brands. Who do you buy this for?

P: Oh, just for myself.

A: No problem. We promise all the products sales on board have higher discount than the duty-free shops.

P: That sounds great. I'd like one pack from Dior and one from Chanel, please.

A: Certainly. If you buy any two packs, you can get an extra $10 voucher, which can be used to buy anything on Air China's flights.

P: It sounds fantastic. I'll have two of them, please. How much are they in total?

A: It's US $110.

P: Here is my credit card.

A: Sure. Your pin number, please.

P: Yes.

A: Here are your two packs of perfume and receipt, please.

P: Thank you so much.

Unit 9 Duty-free Sales

A: You're welcome.

P: Hello, Miss. Can you come over for a while?

A: Yes, Miss. What can I do for you?

P: I saw you have many brands of sunglasses in the brochure. I'd like to buy one for myself. But I am not sure which style fits my face.

A: Generally, we should choose the style of sunglasses which is just the opposite of face shapes. In simple terms, if the face is round, it'd better choose angular ones. And if the face is bit square or long, just choose oval or round ones.

P: That sounds simple. My face is oval.

CA: It's lucky for you. The oval face is suitable for any style. You just need to choose the right color.

P: I'm not sure. Do you have any advice?

A: I think your skin color is just typical Asia color. Natural skin tones suit colors such as black, silver or white. These colors can brighten your skin tone. You can try this black one from Dior. It's better for you.

P: All right. Let me try on.

A: Of course.

P: Oh, both the style and the color look perfect for me. How much is it?

A: It's US $ 345.00.

P: I'll take the black Dior. Here is my credit card.

A: Thank you.

Setting: A man is looking for something in the cart.

A: Good afternoon, Sir. What are you looking for?

P: Well, I'm looking for a wallet that can hold more cards.

A: Oh, we have lots of card clips for men. I'm sure you'll choose the right one for you need.

P: I hope so. Can I see the short black one?

A: Of course. Here is it. This one is a double-story design which can hold up to eight cards.

P: I see. This is still not big enough. Do you have bigger one than this?

A: Yes. I am just about to introduce you another one from Coach which can holds up to 24 cards.

P: That sounds cool. Can you show me the one you said?

A: Certainly I will. Here is it. This one is particularly designed to place cards. I consider this one is much suitable for you.

P: It looks nice. What is this wallet made of?

A: It is made of calfskin so that it's very strong and durable. And it is not expensive. It is the most cost-effective one we have.

P: So how much is it actually?

A: Its original price is US $200.00. Now we have forty percent discount for it. So it's a good deal to buy now.

P: I think so. It seems it's just for me. Please give me one. And here is my credit card.

A: No problem, Sir. Here is your wallet. Hope you enjoy your trip.

P: Thank you very much for your patience.

A: It's my pleasure.

9.3.3 Cultural Background

Fly buys: the world's best airport shops

Julieta Jameson

Got time for a little shopping action pre-holiday flight? Think outside the perfume box and discover some airport specialty stores that perfectly encapsulate the nation outside the arrivals hall.

1. HEATHROW

Harrods

While the legendary Knightsbridge store may carry everything elegant and expensive from Armani to Zegna, you won't find the same range at the airport. But for the lovers of label and slaves to status in your life, you can pick up a Harrods logo mug, bag or teddy bear to stuff in their stocking. There's a good selection of jewelry and customs-ready gourmet food such as chockies and biscuits as well.

2. COPENHAGEN

By Malene Birger

If you're passing through, make sure that you make time for gorgeous Copenhagen Airport. The stylish facility, with its wooden floors and arty lighting, has a fabulous range of shops featuring Scandinavian design.

If we must pick one, it is By Malene Birger, a giant of Danish fashion, making feminine and glam the clean style for which Scandinavia is famous.

3. HONG KONG

Shanghai Tang

Since its creation in the late '90s by Hong Kong businessman David Tang, Shanghai Tang's signature has been opulent brocades, silks, velvet and cashmere. Tang started the label to bring traditional Chinese dress into the modern era, but the luxury brand has been quietly creating a less-ethnic aesthetic. The result is eminently wearable, timeless collections. Teas, chopsticks, tableware and cushion covers make fine gifts too.

4. SINGAPORE CHANGI AIRPORT

TWG Tea Boutique

TWG Tea Boutiques are all the rage with the fashionable young Singaporeans who flock to the Orchard Road emporium to peruse the 20-page tea menu and nibble on macarons. The vintage-inspired packaging and lovely accoutrements make TWG Tea as much about the experience as the brew. The boutique at the airport is purely retail and is a great place to pick up a few packs of such evocatively named blends as Weekend in Shanghai or Silver Moon.

5. FRANKFURT

Omega

Omega may be Swiss but with the outstanding precision of its covetable timepieces, it could be German. This new boutique boasts the entire Omega collection. The most popular offering of 2013: the $US12, 000 ($13,000) "Dark Side of the Moon" Speed master, inspired by and dedicated to the Apollo 8 astronauts.

6. DUBAI

Dubai Duty Free

For a good old-fashioned duty free spree, nowhere beats Dubai's mega-mart. From $1000 bottles of Johnny Walker whisky to $5 phone cards, this is that something-for-everybody place a gift buyer dreams of. You can get a Hugo Boss suit or a Bobby Brown eye shadow; a MacBook or a Mac lipstick. Open 24 hours.

7. SYDNEY INTERNATIONAL AIRPORT

Purely Merino

Don't be put off by the kitsch statue of a shearer at the entrance. Purely Merino is a goldmine for those seeking an easy care wardrobe for travel. Skip the Ugg boots and head for the great range of Metalicus garments as well as various brands of knitwear and other fine wool pieces. Check out hats and gloves, wraps and socks, all made from Australian merino wool.

8. SUVARNABHUMI INTERNATIONAL AIRPORT, BANGKOK

Jim Thompson

Thai silk is legendary and so is Jim Thompson for what he did for it. The former CIA agent turned hotelier of Oriental fame is regarded as being responsible for single-handedly saving the Thai silk industry. Today the name of Thompson who mysteriously disappeared in 1967 is lent to a remarkable empire of fabrics, restaurants and bars. A selection of the lustrous furnishing fabrics and linens is on sale at the airport.

9. SEOUL INCHEON

Cheong-Kwan-Jang

Not all ginsengs are created equal and this brand from the home of the purported wonder plant is said to be the world's best. A general tonic used in Asia for thousands of years to improve health, Cheong-Kwan-Jang, known in English as Korean Ginseng Corp, is the world's biggest seller. It's a plant product though, so quarantine rules apply. Check at the store what forms of ginseng you may bring into Australia.

10. JFK AIRPORT, New York

Coach

As NYC as the Yankees, Coach was founded in 1941, in a Manhattan loft. But at just under 75 square metres, the Coach boutique at New York JFK Airport Terminal 1 is bigger than a lot of NYC lofts and has bags with timeless appeal but enough fashion edge to be interesting.

9.4　Duty-Free Allowances

9.4.1　Language Points and Useful Sentence Patterns

9.4.1.1　Language Points

1. alcoholic drink

a liquor or brew containing alcohol as the active agent

2. IATA

International Air Transport Association

3. cigarette

a thin paper tube of finely cut tobacco for smoking

4. carton

light cardboard or plastic box for holding goods

9.4.1.2　Useful Sentence Patterns

1. Expressing permission

Can/May/Could I have ... ?

I wonder if I could...

Would you mind me doing ... ?

Do you mind if I do ... ?

2. Expressing impermissibility

I'm sorry, but ...

You'd better not ...

I'm afraid you can't ...

You're not allowed ...

9.4.2 Dialogues

Setting: A man who is sitting in the middle of the cabin asking for help.

(P: passenger   A: attendant)

A: Can I help you, Sir?

P: I'd like for bottles of Johnnie Walker Black Label, please?

A: Sorry, Sir. As far as I know, visitors to the United States are allowed one liters of alcoholic drinks at most.

P: Oh, I haven't heard about this.

A: The airline business model for duty-free are encouraged by The International Air Transport Association (IATA), but IATA also set restrictions on duty-free purchase by international airline passengers.

P: Well, since there is such rule, give me one liter, please.

A: No problem, Sir. One liter is about two bottles.

P: Okay, how much are they?

A: It's US $ 35.00 for one bottle. So it's $70 in total.

P: All right. Here is $100, please.

A: Thanks a lot. Here is your drink and $30 change. Hope you enjoy rest of your trip.

P: Thank you very much.

A: It's my pleasure.

Setting: A young lady is looking for something in the cart.

P: Hello, Miss. Can you come over for help?

A: Yes, what can I help you?

P: My husband asked me to buy some cigarettes for him. But I don't know anything about men. Can you give me some advice?

A: We have Marlboro, Benson & Hedges and State Express 555 on this flight. These are all very popular products.

P: I really have no idea for these brands. Which one do you recommend?

A: I have no idea, too. As far as I know, many passengers prefer to buy Marlboro as it is the most famous brand and cost-effective.

P: Okay, I'd like four cartons of Marlboro, please.

A: I'm sorry, Miss. As far as I know, visitors to China are allowed to buy two cartons of cigarettes at most.

P: I haven't heard about this. So can I have two cartons, please?

A: Yes, Miss. Anything else do you need?

P: No, thanks. How much are they?

A: They are 80 dollars. And here ere are your cigarettes.

P: Thanks.

9.4.3 Cultural Background

Duty-Free Allowances

International to international transit passengers may be subject to additional airport security screening at the point of transfer. All duty-free liquids, aerosols and gels may be confiscated if it surpasses maximum limitation and packing requirements. These restrictions may be subject to change without notice.

Country	Alcoholic Beverages	Tobacco, cigarettes or cigars
Australia	2.25 litres (over 18 years)	25 cigarettes (plus an open packet), or 25 grams of tobacco or cigars (over 18 years)
Fiji	2.25 litres of liquor of 4.5 litres of wine or beer (over 17 years)	250 cigarettes or 250 grams of cigars or a combination of tobacco products not exceeding 250 grams (over 17 years)
New Zealand	4.5 litres of wine or; 4.5 litres of beer; 3 bottles (or other containers) each containing not more than 1125ml of spirits, liquer or other spirituous beverages (over 17 years).	50 cigarettes or 50 grams of tobacco or 50 cigars or an assortment of these to a total weight of 50 grams (over 17 years)
Solomons	2 litres of wine or spirits	200 cigarettes or 250g of cigars or 225g of tobacco
Vanuatu	1.5 litres of spirits and 2 litres of wine	200 cigarettes or 100 cigarillos or 50 cigars or 250g of tobacco

9.5 Preorder Duty-free Products on Board

9.5.1 Language Points and Useful Sentence Patterns

9.5.1.1 Language Points

1. preorder

   advanced booking

2. Cashmere

a soft fabric made from the wool of the Cashmere goat

3. stock

the merchandise that a shop has on hand

4. lucky dog

the person who has good luck

5. label

a brief description given for purposes of identification

6. pick up

gather or collect

7. honeymoon

a holiday taken by a newly married couple

9.5.1.2 Useful Sentence Patterns

1. Expressing politeness

Don't mention it.

It's my pleasure.

No worries.

Please don't worry about it.

Not at all.

2. Expressing "No problem"

That's okay/all right.

No problem.

I'll be fine.

Never mind.

9.5.2 Dialogues

(P: passenger   A: attendant)

P: Excuse me, Miss. I saw the Lindt Lindor chocolates on the manual. I'd like to buy some for my little daughter.

A: That's OK. How many packs would you like? There are promotions on our flight. You can get one for free when you buy any five packs of Lindt chocolates.

P: That sounds like a good deal. Can I have ten packs, please?

A: No problem, Sir.

(When the cabin crew checked the cart, suddenly she found that there were only six packs left.)

A: I'm so sorry, Sir. There were only six packs left in this cart. Let my check in the rear cabin. Please wait me for few minutes.

P: That's all right.

(Few minutes past, the cabin crew came back.)

A: I'm so sorry that there were no more packs in the rear cabin. Lindt chocolates are definitely popular. But we do provide pre-order service. You can order the quantity you need on flight, and pick up your goods at our airport store.

P: That sounds like a good idea, too. By the way, how can I do pre-order?

A: You just keep the receipt I give you, and show it to the clerk when you pick up your ordered products.

P: Okay, I will have ten packs, please.

A: Sure, they are US $50.00.

P: Here is my card.

A: Thanks.

Setting: There is about fifty-year-old lady press the call button.

P: Hello, Miss. I'd like this Burberry camel cashmere scarf. How much is it?

A: It's US $400.00. The color you chose is the most classic one of Burberry. But that color is recently out of stock on board. Is there any other colors do you like?

P: The pink one is too young to fit my age. But the black one is too dark.

A: Let me check in the computer to see if there is any at stock.

P: Thank you for that. Hope I am a lucky dog.

(The cabin crew came back from the rear cabin.)

A: I'm glad to tell you there is one camel scarf at our airport store. If you like this color, you can order it here now. I'll let the ground staff to send it to you at the terminal.

P: That will be perfect for me. I'll have this one. Here is my card.

A: Thanks for your understanding. Please keep this receipt and show it to our ground staff.

P: That's great. Thank you for your help.

Setting: There is a young couple talking about buying something.

P: Hello, is there anything I can help out here?

A: Of course. We are looking at these couple's watches. Both of us fancy these CK silver ones. How much are they?

P: Let me have a look.

(The crew checked the product manual.)

A: I'm sorry. The products marked in gray label are only available at our airport stores.

P: Oh, we didn't notice that. So how can we buy these gray label products?

A: These gray label products can be ordered on board and then you can pick them up at our

50

airport stores.

P: But we just started our two-week honeymoon trip to Australia. I am afraid we probably could not pick up the watches soon.

A: Please don't worry about that. We also provide free-delivery service. You can leave your address to me. And I'll ask the ground staff to send your goods directly to your home.

P: Your airline is really thoughtful. We just want this pair of watches.

A: Sure, I'll order for you right now.

P: Thanks a lot. Here is my address.

A: Here is your receipt. Please keep it carefully. If you have any problems, please contact us by calling the number below.

P: Certainly I will.

A: Hope you enjoy your honeymoon in Australia.

P: Thank you so much.

9.5.3 Cultural Background

Airport shopping: Why airport shopping is so hard to avoid
Lee Tulloch

I spend so much time in airports I might as well get to like them. The strange Twilight Zone of departure halls can be strangely comforting if you're in the right frame of mind. The cares of the real world are left behind and all you have to worry about is how long the line will be at your gate. And you know you will be going somewhere. Maybe not soon, but eventually.

These days, airports are not simply places that direct traffic on and off planes but food and beverage hubs, shopping malls and spas. Shrewd airport-owning conglomerates have realized in recent years that they have a captive retail and dining market and so have redesigned the departure areas to make them less about moving people efficiently and more about finding ways to make these same people stop and shop.

Which is not always a good thing? The international airport I spend most time in is Sydney T1 and it's a nightmare. Recent redevelopment of the retail space means that everyone heading to a gate, restaurant or lounge has to first run the gamut of the amorphous new Heinemann Tax and Duty Free outlet.

The departure area always was badly designed. You felt like a pinball in a machine being flung around between perfume sprinklers. But at least there was a (sort of) path through it all, which allowed you to avoid the stands. Now the duty free has swallowed much of the floor and travelers must navigate their own way through the labyrinth before finding clear space to the gates.

Few come out unscathed, having purchased an item they'd never wanted, needed or could afford in the real world. The danger of crashing into people filling wire baskets with bottles in a pre-flight frenzy is high.

Airport retailers bank on the fact that excited travelers leave their good sense behind when they're about to step on a plane. I'm convinced the need to arrive early at check in is not about security but about giving the retailers more time to flog stuff to bored passengers.

But I admit I'm grateful for such distractions when I have a few hours to kill in transit. Some airports are very entertaining, cities unto themselves, and I imagine it would be possible to live in them, even take citizenship if it were allowed.

Heathrow is a case in point. Europe's busiest airport has never been my favorite, but I must say it's very impressive these days. Recently, during a two-hour transit at T5, I met Maria Lourenco, one of Heathrow's Personal Shoppers. I was surprised to hear this is a complimentary service available to everyone, not just those HNW shoppers with a spare zillion pounds to throw around.

The service can be reserved 24-72 hours ahead and, if there's enough transit time, visits can be arranged to shops in different terminals. There's no minimum spend if you don't find anything you like. Heathrow has 15 personal shoppers available, and between them they speak many languages, especially those of rich people—Russians, Chinese and Brazilians. They'll help with fashion advice, styling and gift ideas. Given that Heathrow has just about as many main brands as the London high street (more than 400 retail outlets at last count), if you have an idea what you want, or even if you don't, they'll do the editing for you.

There's also a dedicated lounge where travelers not motivated to move about can view items in comfort. I'm not a fan of shopping at airports because there are few bargains, but the prices of big brands are fairly consistent, so if you know you want that Bally handbag or Thomas Pink shirt, you might as well use your time wisely and buy them at the airport.

Heathrow also has a free Shop & Collect service, where goods purchased on your way in can be collected on departure at a convenient pick up point. Travelers can also reserve items from the Heathrow online boutique and collect and pay for them when they arrive at the airport.

In Australia, it's possible to purchase duty free from an online catalogue ahead of travel, but so far none of our airports are offering free fashion and styling advice.

Lovely Maria and her colleagues can make you feel like a rich person for a couple of hours. And they can help you spend your whole holiday budget before you get on the plane.

Unit 10
Emergency Situations

10.1 Irregular Flight

10.1.1 Language Points and Useful Sentence Patterns

10.1.1.1 Language Points

1. departure

the act of departing

2. schedule

a temporally organized plan for matters to be attended to

3. Air Traffic Control

control of the flow of airplanes

4. irregular

not occurring at expected times

5. connecting flight

a flight with an intermediate stop and a change of aircraft (possibly a change of airlines)

6. typhoon

a very violent tropical storm with a circular wind in the western Pacific

7. mechanical

relating to or concerned with machinery or tools

8. overnight

lasting, open, or operating through the whole night

10.1.1.2 Useful Sentence Patterns

1. Expressing regret

I'm so/really/very/terribly sorry about that...

I do apologize about that ...

Please accept my sincere apology.

We are so sorry to do ...

What ridiculous you are!

It sounds unbelievable.

I'm so disappointment with something.

2. Expressing complaint

I'm afraid I have a complaint to make.

Saying that you're dissatisfied with something ...

I'm so pissed off with your attitude.

This is too much.

This is more than I can take.

I've had enough of that.

10.1.2 Dialogues

(P: passenger   GS: ground staff)

Setting: It's already 10:00 a.m., one hour after scheduled departure time of Flight CZ3396 from Zhengzhou to Guangzhou, yet it has not been informed to board. Passengers are still waiting in the waiting hall.

P: Excuse me, the scheduled departure time of my flight was 9:00 a.m.. It's already one hour late. What's wrong with our flight?

GS: We're so sorry, madam. We were just informed that your flight has been delayed due to air traffic control.

P: What ridiculous you are. You let us wait here for nearly one hour without any announcement. I got a very important meet to attend this afternoon.

GS: We do apologize for the irregular flight.

P: Why can't we take off? The weather condition at this airport seems normal.

GS: The delay was due to air traffic control.

P: I'm sorry. It's hard for me to understand this situation. The flight cannot take off under such great air condition.

GS: I'm terribly sorry that I haven't made myself understood. Your flight can not take off due to air traffic control.

P: How can I believe you?

GS: Madam, I am sorry to hear that. We got the information from airport traffic control department. If you have any question, you may seek legal means to protect your rights.

P: That's fine. By the way, when will my flight departure?

GS: Sorry, madam. I'm not sure the new departure time. We'll take off once we receive the permission from the airport ground department.

P: It sounds I have to wait.

GS: I feel bad about that too. We provide some tea and coffee. Pleased take your seat and get something to drink.

P: Excuse me. I just heard from the airport announcement that my flight has been canceled due to the heavy storm at the destination airport.

GS: Yes, Sir. All flight flying to Guangzhou has been canceled due to Super Typhoon Yutu. The aircraft cannot land down there.

P: It sounds too bad. I got a connecting flight at Guangzhou Baiyun International Airport tomorrow afternoon. What should I do now?

GS: You'd better refund your ticket and go to Guangzhou by train. Or you can change your connecting flight in the meantime.

P: Do I have to pay for the ticket rescheduling?

GS: Of course not. You are able to change your flight for free due to the bad weather.

P: So when will our flight take off?

GS: The new departure time is still uncertain. We'll update the information every 30 minutes.

P: I think I'd better refund my ticket and change train to Guangzhou.

GS: I'm sorry about the inconvenience that caused.

P: Where is the ticket counter?

GS: Just go ahead and the ticket counter is down there on your left.

P: Thank you very much.

GS: Sorry again.

(Announcement: Passengers for flight CA1316, attention please: we are sorry to inform you that your flight has been delayed due to mechanical reasons. Please remain in the waiting hall and wait for further information.)

P: Excuse me, Miss. I've just heard from the announcement that my flight has been canceled due to mechanical reasons. It means I can't flight today.

GS: We're so sorry about the inconvenience caused. We've just been informed your flight has been canceled due to mechanical problems.

P: It sounds unbelievable. Airplanes are the most safety transport in the world. How did these problems happen?

GS: Don't worry about that, Sir. We will change another aircraft if the problems can't be fixed up. Unfortunately you have to stay over in the hotel.

P: I am so disappointed with your company.

GS: Please accept my sincere apology. We will offer you the accommodation and meal because of the inconvenience we caused. Please bring your overnight articles and valuables with you. Our ground staff will show you where the buses are.

P: Okay, I hope I would fly tomorrow.

GS: We are so sorry to make so much trouble to you. Hope you could enjoy your stay tonight.

P: That's all right. I hope I could fly as soon as possible.

10.1.3 Cultural Background

Top 5 Flight Delays Slowing Down Your Airline This Fall

Travelers do everything they can to make their time spent with your airline the shortest it can be. They get to the airport early, use mobile check-in and even opt for TSA pre-check just so they can get from Point A to Point B as quickly and painlessly as possible. When the top priorities of your customers are speed and safety, it's no wonder why the inconvenience of flight delays can distract your travelers from the safety concerns behind the wait.

While flight delays are an inconvenience for fliers, they can be just as much of a hassle for airlines themselves. Both in-person and social media backlash can be fierce and quick from angry travelers affected by delays. The best way to handle flight delays is to inform your staff, to not give out false information to travelers and to understand the most common reasons behind delays.

	Percent of Total Delay Minutes												
	2003 (Jun-Dec)	2004	2005	2006	2007	2008	2009	2010	2011	2012	2013	2014	2015
Air Carrier Delay	26.3%	25.8%	28.0%	27.8%	28.5%	27.8%	28.0%	30.4%	30.1%	31.9%	29.4%	30.2%	32.2%
Aircraft Arriving Late	30.9%	33.6%	34.2%	37.0%	37.7%	36.6%	36.2%	39.4%	40.8%	41.4%	42.1%	41.9%	39.8%
Security Delay	0.3%	0.3%	0.2%	0.3%	0.2%	0.1%	0.1%	0.2%	0.1%	0.1%	0.1%	0.1%	0.1%
National Aviation System Delay	36.5%	33.5%	31.4%	29.4%	27.9%	30.2%	30.6%	25.7%	24.8%	22.5%	24.2%	23.5%	22.9%
Extreme Weather	6.1%	6.9%	6.2%	5.6%	5.7%	5.4%	5.0%	4.4%	4.1%	4.0%	4.1%	4.3%	5.0%

SOURCE: Bureau of Transportation Statistics

US Airport Security, the Independent

The least common reason for flight delays is security. Terminal or concourse evacuations, re-boarding of aircraft's after a security breach, inoperative screen equipment and long lines all count for security delays. Only 0.1% of all delays in 2015 were due to security delays, but it's still important to be prepared for this rare set-back.

Extreme weather consists of weather conditions that prevent aircrafts from flying. These are significant meteorological conditions that delay or prevent the operation of a flight, such as: tornadoes, blizzards, hurricanes or cyclones. Extreme weather delays accounted for 5% of all delays in 2015. Airlines can pay attention to the latest meteorological reports on these conditions or even employ a team of meteorologists to keep them up to date on the latest severe weather systems.

National Aviation System (NAS) Delays are any delays attributed to the broad set of conditions as outlined by the NAS and normally account for about 22% of all airport hold-ups. These conditions are classified as non-extreme weather events, airport operation issues, heavy traffic volume and issues with air traffic control. This category of delays consists of weather conditions that slow operations down and can be reduced with corrective actions taken by the airports or the Federal Aviation Administration. Hail that diverted a landing for an Air Canada flight would fall into this category.

Air-traffic

The second most common flight delay comes from air carrier delays. Any time a delay is out of your control as an airline it is known as an air carrier delay. These are quite common; in fact, they made up 32.3% of all delays in 2015. When maintenance or crew problems, aircraft cleaning, baggage loading or fueling is holding your airline's operations up, it is an aircraft carrier delay and it is important to let your travelers know the status of their flights as quickly as possible.

Unit 10　Emergency Situations

Aircraft-late

The top reason for flight delays impacting airlines is simply an aircraft arriving late. This has consistently been the number one reason for flight delays for over a decade. In 2015, nearly 40% of all delays were due to an aircraft being late. While a late aircraft can have a ripple effect throughout your airlines daily itinerary, this delay poses the least amount of safety concerns for your passengers.

10.2　Experiencing Turbulence

10.2.1　Language Points and Useful Sentence Patterns

10.2.1.1　Language Points

1. turbulence

instability in the atmosphere

2. bump

knock against with force or violence

3. chop

the irregular motion of waves (usually caused by wind blowing in a direction opposite to the tide)

4. ankle

a gliding joint between the distal ends of the tibia and fibula and the proximal end of the talus

5. fracture

breaking of hard tissue such as bone

6. first-aid kit

kit consisting of a set of bandages and medicines for giving first aid

7. swell

increase in size, magnitude, number, or intensity

10.2.1.2　Useful Sentence Patterns

1. Inquiring situation

What's up?

What's happening?

How are you going?

How are things with you?

What's the matter with you?

What's wrong with you?

2. Expressing uncomfortable

I'm feeling rather bad.

I feel drowsy, dizzy and nauseated.

I feel lighted-headed.

My head is pounding.

The headache is killing me.

10.2.2　Dialogues

(P: Passenger   A: Attendant)

(Announcement: Ladies and Gentleman: our flight is experiencing turbulence, please remain in your seat and fasten your seat belt. The toilet cannot be used during turbulence. Thank you!)

P: Excuse me, Miss. Why is our airplane bumping so hard?

A: Sir, we are experiencing turbulence, which is that bumpy, choppy sensation as you feel at the moment. Please fasten your seat belt.

P: What did you mean that? You mean our plane is unsafe now.

A: It's not so unsafe as you think. Turbulence is normal and happens quiet often. It is just air movement and can range from slight to severe bouncing, pitching and rolling. It can be dangerous. However, airplanes are built to withstand these conditions. So please remain calm and wear your seat belt.

P: I feel uncomfortable when I wear the seat belt.

A: For your safety, please follow the cabin crew's instruction.

P: Okay. Thank you for reminding me.

A: Never mind.

(While a passenger is waiting outside the lavatory in the aisle, the cabin broadcast is on.)

A: Excuse me, Madam. Our plane is experiencing turbulence. For your safety, please go back to your seat and fasten your seat belt.

P: That's ridiculous. I am waiting here for a few minutes. I can't wait to go to the bathroom.

A: I do understand your situation. But according to the safety instruction, the lavatory must be closed during turbulence in order to avoid unnecessary injuries.

P: I don't need too much time. And the plane is just slightly bumping at the moment.

A: Madam, you can sit in the seat next to you and keep the seat belt fasten. When the 'fasten seat belt sign' is off, you can use the bathroom.

P: That's fine. It seems I have to wait.

A: Thank you for your understanding and cooperation. The turbulence won't be long.

P: No problem.

Setting: When the cabin attendants are providing meal and drink in the cabin, the airplane suddenly shook violently.

P: Excuse me, Miss. Your trolley hit my ankle.

A1: I'm so sorry, Sir. Please let me check your ankle. How are you feeling now?

(One of the cabin attendant came to check the passenger's injury, the other one went back to get the first-aid kit.)

P: My left ankle hurts so much.

A1: Sir, I am terribly sorry to hear that. Could you try to turn it around? I need to make sure whether the bones are broken or not.

(The man tried to turn the ankle a little bit.)

P: Oh, God. It's actually painful. But I think I am still able to control my foot.

A1: It's good to hear that. Judging from the current situation, your ankle should not be fractured.

(The cabin attendant got the first aid kit.)

A2: Sir, please let me treat your injury with a bandage to prevent further injury. And I'll put the ice pack on your foot in case it swells.

P: Thank you for your careful treatment.

A2: We'll keep a close audience for your situation. If you have any uncomfortable, please don't hesitate to contact us.

P: Sure, will. Don't worry too much about me.

A2: The ambulance will wait on the apron and take you to the hospital for further examination.

61

P: Thanks anyway.

A2: Sorry again.

10.2.3 Cultural Background

FLIGHT DELAY COMPENSATION

Ever experienced 3 hours'flight delay? If yes, then according to the European Union Regulation EC 261/2004, you have the right to ask for compensation. This amount is up to $700 (€600) per person.

The European Commission (EC) introduced Regulation No. 261 in 2004 to care for air passengers. The compensation is up to 600 Euros for flight delays, cancellations and denied boarding.

You are eligible for compensation if …

➢ You arrived with a delay of 3 hours or more at the final destination.

➢ You departed from an EU airport, or landed at an EU airport with an EU regulated airline.

For the record, 'arrival time' is registered when the aircraft lands and one of its doors opens. But the airlines usually try to amend this rule.

They argue that as soon as the aircraft hits the runway is the arrival time. Don't be surprised, companies love exploiting loopholes in the system. The good thing is you do not have to be an EU citizen to claim. Flight delay occurs, and it is a common thing for air travelers. But, it's important to know your rights in case you face one. This way you would know what you are entitled to. It can be due to so many reasons. The airlines are not responsible for all of them.

Can airlines have control over storms and extreme weather conditions? No, but they can be responsible for things under control like technical faults or mishandling aircrew. Simply put, if the delay could have been avoided, the airline owes you money. By the way, the stats are on your side. Looking at historical data the airlines have been responsible for most of these. This is good news.

The US and the EU have different policies for the air passengers. The EU gives more rights to air travelers. You could also say that it puts more pressure on the airlines. But you should know how it works. Strangely, not many people knew that they can claim money from the airlines. It is like leaving cash on the table. So think of this 'explanatory guide' as an awareness post.

AMOUNT OF COMPENSATION

The compensation amount varies depending on the length of the delay and route distance. You can use our free compensation calculator to check the compensation amount that the airline owes you. Enter your flight number and travel date in the compensation checker tool and the exact amount will pop right up.

The rule is simple. To claim money back, you should have reached later than 3 hours at your final destination. The following table is a snippet of the amounts you can expect in Euros (€) from airlines under the EU Regulation 261/2004.

ARRIVAL DELAY	ROUTE DISTANCE	COMPENSATION
Up to 2 hours 59 mins	Any distance	None
3 hours or more	less than or equal to 1500 km	€250
	more than 1500 km within EU	€400
	1500 to 3500 km	€400
3 to 4 hours	over 3500 km	€300*
over 4 hours	over 3500 km	€600

We have dealt with thousands of flight disruption cases. And have received reimbursement up to €600 for each customer. With a 99%-win record, we can confidently say that we will get your cash back.

To calculate the route distance, you can use the Great Circle Mapper Tool. It is an online tool to calculate the route distance. Simply enter your departure and arrival airport and that is it.

AM I ENTITLED TO COMPENSATION FOR A DELAYED FLIGHT?

Under the EU Law (EC 261 of 2004), to be eligible for compensation;

➢ You must have arrived later than 3 hours at your final destination.
➢ Your flight must have departed from an EU airport or landed at an EU airport with the airline headquartered in an EU country.
➢ Flight disruption should not be caused due to extraordinary circumstances or situations beyond the control of airlines.
➢ You checked in on time (i.e., 45 minutes before departure time.)

EU covers 28 countries, including the Canary Islands, Iceland and Azores. Bear in mind that the Channel Islands, Isle of Man and Faroe Islands are not covered. To read details about your rights for short haul, medium haul or long haul flights, you can visit UK's Civil Aviation Authority Website.

Let's use a simple example.

Your original flight was from Los Angeles to London with British Airways, or from Munich to New York with American Airlines, but landed after a delay of over 4 hours. In both these cases, you have the right to ask for compensation.

WHAT ARE EXCEPTIONAL CIRCUMSTANCES? CAN I CLAIM COMPENSATION FOR DELAYS DUE TO EXTRAORDINARY CIRCUMSTANCES?

There are exceptional (extraordinary) circumstances under which you are not eligible for compensation.

These are:

➢ Natural disasters such as Earthquake, Tsunami, bad weather, lightning strikes, and volcanic eruptions
➢ Air traffic control restrictions

- Crew members strike
- Political unrest
- Technical issues caused due to a bird hitting the plane engine

The table given below clarifies when a passenger can or cannot demand compensation when it comes to exceptional circumstances:

CIRCUMSTANCE	STRIKE	NATURAL DISASTERS	TECHNICAL PROBLEM
Circumstances which couldn't be avoided	A strike is an exceptional circumstance	Earthquake, Tsunami, Extreme weather, Volcanic eruption is natural disasters and cannot be controlled	If happens on a broader scale, for example, closure of airport due to the technical problem
Ordinary circumstances when airlines may pay compensation	If any other airline was operational during strike	If the runway was not cleared.	If it could be avoided, for example by catching birds at the runway or keeping spare parts

Note: Strike is only considered as extraordinary if all flights traveling the same day are canceled or delayed. However, if other airlines were operational then you can ask for compensation.

10.3 Sick Passengers on Board

10.3.1 Language Points and Useful Sentence Patterns

10.3.1.1 Language Points

1. dizzy

having or showing an unpleasant feeling that things are going round and round

2. nauseous

causing or able to cause nausea

3. vomit

the matter ejected in vomiting

4. symptom

any sensation or change in bodily function that is experienced by a patient and is associated with a particular disease

5. painkiller

a medicine used to relieve pain

6. formula

a liquid food for infants

7. thermometer

measuring instrument for measuring temperature

8. fever

a rise in the temperature of the body

10.3.1.2 Useful Sentence Patterns

1. Expressing the hope of removal of disabilities

Hope you get well soon !

I hope you will soon recover.

I hope you'll be well soon.

We sincerely hope that you will soon be restored to health.

2. Expressing airsickness

I'm afraid I got airsick.

I've got dizziness and nausea, and feel like vomiting.

I'm feeling dizzy and nauseous.

I think I am a little bit airsick.

I have got a severe headache since the airplane took off.

10.3.2 Dialogues

(P: passenger   A: attendant)

A: Did you press the call button, Madam? What's the matter?

P: I'm feeling dizzy and nauseous.

A: What did you have in the morning, Madam?

P: I just had some bread and milk in a bit rush before I went to the airport.

A: That's why you're feeling uncomfortable now. I think you're suffering airsickness.

P: Could you bring me some water, please?

A: Sure, just a moment, Madam.

P: And can I have an extra airsickness bag, too?

A: No problem, Madam. I'll be back in a minute.

(Suddenly the passenger vomits into the sick bag.)

P: I'm sorry for the mess, Miss.

A: It doesn't matter, Madam. Let me dispose the bag for you. Did you feel better now? Shall I bring some airsickness tablets for you?

P: No, thanks. I feel much better now. I just want to have some sleep.

A: Okay, here are your water and sickness bags. Some sleep does help to relieve symptoms. You'd better fasten your seat belt in case the "Fasten seat belt sign" turns on. The weather on the airway is not very good today.

P: Thank you very much for your kindness help.

A: It's my pleasure.

P: Hello, Miss. Could you come here for a while?

A: What can I do for you, Madam?

P: I have got a severe headache since the airplane took off. And it's even getting worse.

A: Oh, I'm sorry to hear that, Madam. Would you like me to lean your seat back and have a rest?

P: I really appreciated what you've done for me. I tried to sleep, but it didn't work at all. Can I have some painkillers, please? I can't stand any more.

A: What's medicine you usually take? I'll see if we have any.

P: Aspirin will be fine. And a cup of hot water, please.

A: No, problem, just a moment, please.

(The cabin attendant came back after two minutes)

A: Here's the water and medicine, Madam.

P: Thanks.

A: You're welcome. The airflow knob is over your head. You can adjust it to get the fresh air. I hope you will get better soon.

P: I hope so. Thank you so much. It's considerate of you.

A: Take care.

Setting: While the cabin attendants are cleaning up in the cabin, a baby is crying all the time. The cabin attendant just came up for help.

A: Hello, Madam. Is there anything needs help?

P: Well, my baby can't stop crying. I just fed him 200 milliliter formula half an hour before. I don't think he cried because of hunger.

A: I think so. Sometimes babies feel uncomfortable because of the air pressure change. You can try to give him some water and see if he can feel better.

(Ten minutes passed, but the baby is still crying without stop.)

P: Excuse me, Miss. Can you come over for a while?

A: Sure, how can I help you here?

P: My son still keeps crying. His chin turned red. I'm afraid he got a fever. Do you have the thermometer on board? I need to take his temperature.

A: No problem, madam. I'll get it for you and come back soon.

(The cabin attendant took the thermometer back.)

A: Here you are, Madam.

P: Thanks a lot.

(The madam took her son's temperature. He had a temperature of almost 39 degrees centigrade.)

P: My son had a fever. Do you have any medicine on board?

A: I'm so sorry, Madam. We don't have medicine for little babies. We just have tablets. But we have the ice bag which can be used to reduce the temperature, too. Meanwhile, you'd better loosen his coat and he can breathe smoothly.

P: It's really thoughtful of you. I even don't know what I should do without your help.

A: We are responsible for every passenger. If you have anything need to help, please don't feel hesitate to contact us.

P: Certainly. Thank you so much.

A: You're welcome.

10.3.3 Cultural Background

What Happens During an In-Air Medical Emergency?

Scary as it may seem, experiencing a serious health incident when you're in-air is actually pretty uncommon. Medical emergencies occur in roughly 1 out of 600 commercial flights, according to findings published in the New England Journal of Medicine. And there's no evidence that the act of flying makes serious health problems like stroke or heart attack more likely, says Christian Martin-Gill, M.D., an assistant professor of emergency medicine at the University of Pittsburgh, who consults with airlines from the ground in the event of a medical emergency.

Still, if something serious does happen, you're in good hands—even if there's no doctor actually on board. "There's some variability between airlines, but the FAA (Federal Aviation Administration) requires flight attendants to be trained in using an external defibrillator and in basic first aid," says Martin-Gill. That means that they'd be able to provide immediate treatment for a heart attack or stroke. They can also handle things like minor injuries or lightheadedness caused by dehydration.

But if a flight attendant can't solve a problem on his own—or if they see signs of a serious issue, like fainting or heavy bleeding—he can call in reinforcements. Airlines coordinate with 24-hour medical call centers like the University of Pittsburgh's STAT-MD Communications Center. When the flight crew calls in, they can connect with a consulting physician like Dr. Martin-Gill to make a diagnosis and decide on a treatment plan. "We discuss the situation with the pilot or attendant to figure out what's going on with the patient," he says. "Then we'll come up with a list of recommendations."

Treatment could be something simple—like having a lightheaded passenger drink some water. It could also involve administering drugs from the plane's on-board medical kit. These kits include things like epinephrine or antihistamine for allergic reactions, anticonvulsants for seizures, nitroglycerin tablets for chest pain, or even meds to deal with postpartum bleeding if a woman gives birth during a flight.

When the situation is really serious—like in the case of a heart attack, stroke, cardiac arrest, or seizure—the flight crew and the consulting physician, along with dispatchers on the ground, decide if the plane should make an emergency landing.

When that happens, 911 are notified, so an ambulance is ready and waiting to take the patient to the hospital when the plane touches down.

10.4 Alternative landing

10.4.1 Language Points and Useful Sentence Patterns

10.4.1.1 Language Points

1. pale
   highly diluted with white
2. abdomen
   the region of the body of a vertebrate between the thorax and the pelvis
3. quadrant
   a measuring instrument for measuring altitude of heavenly bodies
4. appendicitis
   inflammation of the vermiform appendix
5. alternative landing
   serving or used in place of another airports

10.4.1.2 Useful Sentence Patterns

1. Expressing painful

   I have acute pain in ...
   I had burning sensation in my stomach.
   I'm experiencing sharp pains in ...
   I felt a series of stabbing pains coming from ...
   I've had this thumping headache since ...

2. Expressing understanding

   I realize how difficult it's going to be, but we must try.
   Can you make sense of what I say?
   I appreciate that it's a difficult decision for you to make.
   I think I got the gist of what she was saying.
   I know how you feel.

I totally understand you.

10.4.2 Dialogues

(P: passenger   A: attendant)

Setting: While flight attendants are providing meals to passengers in the cabin, there is a passenger who just called for help.

A: Hello, Sir. What's the matter with you? Your face is rather pale.

P: I have no idea what is going on. I just got a sudden pain in my abdomen.

A: Could you show me where exactly the pain is?

P: It's here, just in the right lower quadrant.

A: Do you feel better when you press it?

P: Yes, that's why I did so. Do you know what my trouble is?

A: I'm not sure. Would you tell me more details about your symptoms? Like what had you done just now and before you got on board?

P: Um... There's nothing special. I just drove my son to school early in the morning as what I do every day. Then I hurried to the airport. On the way, I dropped in a restaurant and had a cheese burger with some salad in a bit hurry. When I arrived at the airport, I just felt a little bit stomachache. I thought it could have gotten better as I was seated on board. Unfortunately, the pain is getting worse, especially in the right lower quadrant. I can't stand any more.

A: It's clear enough. Now I need to take your temperature. Please lay down and relax.

(After five minutes, the attendant takes out the thermometer to check the temperature.)

A: Sir, I'm afraid you have a fever. Depending on your symptoms, I can basically judge that you may have appendicitis.

P: My goodness. What should I do about it?

A: Calm down. Sir. I am going to report to the pursuer. At the same time, I'll see if there is a doctor or nurse on board through the broadcasting system.

(The attendant reported the man's condition to the purser. The purser soon makes a sick announcement: Ladies and Gentlemen, May I have your attention, please? There is a sick passenger on board. If there is a doctor or a nurse on this flight, please contact any of our cabin attendants immediately. Thank you.)

(A few minutes past, no one contacts them. So the purser reports to the captain.)

A: I'm sorry to tell you that there is no doctor on this flight. According to your condition, the captain has decided to land at an alternative airport nearby. We have informed the ground medical department. The ambulance will meet our plane at the apron. You will receive the timely treatment when you disembark. Please have a bit of patience.

P: Thank you very much for your help.

A: Not at all.

Announcement: Ladies and Gentlemen, I'm the captain of this flight. I's so sorry to inform you that our flight is about to make an alternative landing at Nanyang Jiangying Airport after 30 minutes due to dense fog at Xinzheng International Airport.

P: Excuse me, Miss. I just heard from the announcement our flight will not be landing at Zhengzhou. Where will we land tonight?

A: I'm sorry, Sir. The destination airport is closed due to poor visibility. Our flight has prepared for landing at Nanyang Jiangying Airport.

P: Oh, dear. Why is this happening? I have to work on Monday.

A: We do apologize for the inconvenience. According to CAAC's regulation, airplanes are not allowed to take off or land if the visibility standard is lower than 800 meters.

P: I'm afraid I have to complain you about this.

A: Sir, I do understand how you are feeling now. However, to make sure passengers' safety, every airline company must comply with the standard made by CAAC. I hope you can understand.

P: When will we fly again?

A: We're not sure the exact new take-off time. Please follow the instruction of the cabin crew. Our company will arrange everything for you.

P: It seems I have to stay here tonight.

A: Thank you for your understanding and cooperation. Hope you have a good night tonight.

P: I hope the weather will be fine for flight tomorrow.

10.4.3 Cultural Background

How to Perform CPR

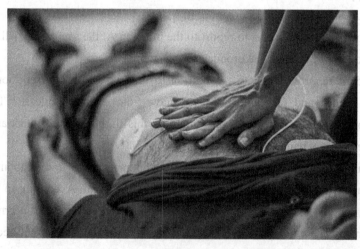

Sudden cardiac arrest occurs when the heart unexpectedly stops beating, which cuts off blood flow to the brain and other organs. If not treated, it can cause death within minutes.

In fact, only about 10 percent of people overall who experience it outside a hospital survive with their brain functions intact, a new study in JAMA found.

But early action can stave off the Grim Reaper: When sudden cardiac arrest victims first received CPR from bystanders, they were more likely to survive with favorable prognoses, the researchers discovered.

But the way you perform CPR has changed in recent years. You no longer have to put your mouth on the victim's.

Regular, non-medical folks who perform CPR on adult cardiac arrest victims are actually more successful if they don't include mouth-to-mouth breaths, says Vinay Nadkarni, M.D., spokesperson for the American Heart Association (AHA).

People who perform compression-only CPR may initiate it more quickly, as well as deliver more chest compressions with fewer interruptions, according to an AHA report in Circulation.

How to Perform CPR the Right Way

Before you do anything, call 911 first. Then perform compression-only CPR. Kneel over the person, placing the heel of your hand on the middle of his or her chest. Put your other hand on top. Then, push hard and fast, pumping down to the beat of the song "Staying' Alive" by the Bee Gees.

The tempo of the song is 100 beats per minute, which is just fast enough to keep circulating oxygen that's already in the patient's body, basically doing the work of the heart.

CPR is a workout, and even an athletic guy will start to wear out from compressions after 2 minutes, says Dr. Nadkarni. But don't try to pace yourself—maintaining speed and force is crucial. Instead, see if another bystander could take over until help arrives—or until you're ready to get back in there.

Unit 11
Transfer Service

11.1 Transferring Guidance

11.1.1 Language Points and Useful Sentence Patterns

11.1.1.1 Language Points

1. non-stop flight

a flight with no intermediate stops

2. transit

people change flights and wait during different stages of a journey

3. direct flight

a flight with one or more intermediate stops but no change of aircraft

4. destination

the place where someone is going or where something is being sent or taken

5. recheck in

when you recheck in at an airport, you show your ticket before going on the connecting flight

6. board

when you board a train, ship, or aircraft, you get on it in order to travel somewhere

7. connecting flight

a flight with an intermediate stop and a change of aircraft (possibly a change of airlines)

8. credential

a document attesting to the truth of certain stated facts

9. corresponding

having the same or nearly the same relationship

10. thoughtful

if you describe someone as thoughtful, you approve of them because they remember what other people want, need, or feel, and try not to upset them

11.1.1.2 Useful Sentence Patterns

Asking for help

Excuse me, can you tell me where to transfer?

Where can I get information on a connecting flight?

Where is the transfer counter for …?

Excuse me, where can I transfer?

I can't find the connecting counter.

Do you know any restaurant or shops nearby?

Unit 11　Transfer Service

Do you know where to eat nearby? I have to wait for … hours before transferring.
Are there any duty-free shops in the transit lounge?
Go straight, and turn left, then you will see the transfer counter.
Go to the connecting counter on the … floor.
Go to the transfer counter for further information.
Please go to the counter and get the boarding pass for your connecting flight first.
It's near …
There is a … near …
Yes. You can find a … near …

11.1.2　Dialogues

(G: Ground Staff　P: Passenger)

P: Excuse me, I have problem here.

G: Yes, how can I help you?

P: I thought what I tool was a "non-stop flight". Why do I have to transit here?

G: I'm sorry, Sir. Your ticket shows that your flight will fly directly to Los Angeles. You don't have to change flights, but you do have to stop over here for about two hours.

P: I am a little confused. Do you mean "non-stop flight" and "direct flight" are not the same?

G: No, they aren't. Non-stop flights won't make any stops during the flight.

P: What about direct flights?

G: Direct flights just mean you don't have to make any connection on the way to the destination.

P: Oh. Now I see. Well, if I had to transfer here and continue my journey to Los Angeles, what should I do?

G: Then, you would have to go to the Transfer Counter and recheck in.

P: Will I get a new boarding pass?

G: Yes, you will.

P: Thank you for your detailed explanation. Now, how long should I wait here?

G: About two hours.

P: Since there are still two hours to wait, could you show me some place to have a drink?

G: Sure. Can you see the sign over here?

P: Yes. The yellow one?

G: Right. Just go straight and then turn right. You will see a coffee shop right on your left.

P: I see. When do we board again?

G: Your flight will depart at 6 p.m. However, you might need to get ready for boarding 40 minutes before the departure.

P: Alright. Thank you very much for your help.

P: Excuse me. I need to take the connecting flight to Paris, but I don't know what to do now, can you help me?

G: Yes. You just got off the first flight, didn't you?

P: Yes, and then I came here directly.

G: OK, what you should do now is to find the connecting flight counter.

P: Can you tell me how to get there? I'm easy to get lost in a strange place.

G: Sure. The connecting flight counter is on the second floor of the terminal building. It's in front of you when you get to the second floor by the elevator.

P: Oh, great. And then they will tell me what to do?

G: They will give you your ticket of the connecting flight after you give them your credentials.

P: Then I can go to get on the plane?

G: No. Can you tell me when will the connecting flight arrive?

P: About 10:30.

G: It's 8:30 now. So the boarding time is in about one hour. After you get your ticket, you need to find the corresponding waiting lounge and sit for almost an hour.

P: Great. To tell you the truth, I'm a little bit tired now.

G: You can have a good rest in the waiting lounge. There are drinks and food there.

P: Yes. It's very thoughtful of you. Oh, right. What about my luggage? Need I to collect my luggage now?

G: No, you don't have to. The cargo aircraft will take your luggage to your destination. So you don't worry about that.

P: Great. Then I will be more relaxed. Thank you very much.

G: My pleasure. Have a nice trip.

11.1.3 Cultural Background

Matters needing attention for passengers of transfer flights

Connecting passengers should pay attention to the connecting time between flights when they buy tickets. The connecting time between domestic flights shall not be less than 2 hours, and the connecting time between domestic and international flights shall not be less than 3 hours.

If passengers transfer at regular airports, please try to take the luggage along as much as possible. Some airports have transfer counters, which can be used to handle boarding pass the next section directly. But most of the counters cannot handle check-in luggage. If passengers have check-in luggage, you need to go to the baggage lobby to pick up the baggage, and then go to the departure lobby to re-check the boarding pass, and then go through security check.

In Beijing, Shanghai, Shenzhen and other large airports, the transfer and luggage check can be directly handled within the airport. After landing, passengers can ask the airport service personnel how to handle.

11.2 At the Transfer Counter

11.2.1 Language Points and Useful Sentence Patterns

11.2.1.1 Language Points

1. transfer

if you transfer or are transferred when you are on a journey, you change from one vehicle to another.

2. formalities

formal actions or procedures that are carried out as part of a particular activity or event

3. staff

the staff of an organization are the people who work for it.

4. lounge

in an airport, a lounge is a very large room where people can sit and wait for aircraft to arrive or leave.

5. connection

if you get a connection at an airport, you catch a plane, after getting off another plane, in order to continue your journey.

6. tolerable

if you describe something as tolerable, you mean that you can bear it, even though it is unpleasant or painful.

7. necessary

something that is necessary is needed in order for something else to happen.

11.2.1.2 Useful Sentence Patterns

Asking for help

I'm connecting with …

What time is the connecting flight?

How much time do we have to transfer?

Could you please explain the process of making a connection?

Could you please explain what should I need for the connecting flight?

Where is the boarding gate for …?

Which gate is for the connecting flight?

Do I have to claim and transfer my baggage again?

Replies:

May I have your boarding pass for the connecting flight?

… later after you arrive at …

There're still … hours to go.

You have to go through all the formalities again when you transfer to the connecting flight.

Gate …, straight ahead.

You should go to Gate ….

Please take the shuttle bus for your connecting flight.

You don't have to claim and transfer your baggage.

Your baggage will be transferred to the connecting flight automatically.

11.2.2 Dialogues

(G: Ground Staff   P: Passenger)

G: Good morning, Sir. Can I help you?

P: Good morning. I'm transferring to Shanghai on flight CA1897. What should I do now?

G: Please go to the transit counter on the ground floor to go through the connecting formalities.

P: Do I have to change my boarding pass there?

G: Yes. Our staff at the transit counter will help you.

P: You mean I have deal with all the formalities again?

G: I'm afraid so.

(Found the transit lounge and go to the connecting counter)

P: Hello, I'm the passenger for flight CA1897. Is this the right counter to check in at?

G: Yes, How can I help you?

P: I have to make a connection to Shanghai at 7:00.

G: OK. Can I have your passport and your ticket?

P: Sure, here you are.

G: Let me check. Mr. Li, right?

P: Yes, that's me.

G: Here is your boarding pass.

P: Thank you. Which gate?

G: Gate 27.

(T: Ticket Clerk   G: Ground Staff   P: Passenger)

(At the Ticket Office)

P: Is that a direct flight?

T: Sorry, there is no direct flight, I'm afraid you have to transfer at New York.

P: Oh no, I hate to wait in the airport for the connecting flight.

T: You have to wait only for 30 minutes.

P: 30 minutes. Oh, that's tolerable.

T: So should I book this ticket for you?

P: OK.

(At the Transit Counter)

P: Excuse me. Is this the transfer counter?

G: Yes, Sir. How may I help you?

P: I just came in on flight 237 and I am transferring to Los Angeles. Do I have to change planes?

G: May I see your boarding pass, Sir?

P: Sure. Here it is.

G: You are going to Los Angeles on flight 237, so you don't have to change planes.

P: Do I have time to make a phone call?

G: Yes, you have half an hour. Just be at Gate 12 for boarding at 12:35.

P: Do I need to check in again?

G: No, that is not necessary.

P: Thank you.

11.2.3 Cultural Background

Study: Asia's airports among world's top 20 most connected

According to the recently released International Megahubs Index 2018, six Asian airports have been ranked among the top 20 most connected airports worldwide.

Released by OAG, the index looks at airports with the highest ratio of scheduled international connections to the number of destinations served.

"The top 50 International megahubs are those airports with the highest ratio of possible scheduled international connections to the number of destinations served by the airport," OAG explained.

"Online and interline connections are included and utilizing the power of Connections Analyzer, low-cost carriers (LCC) connections are also included."

The largest megahubs in Asia-Pacific are all located in Southeast Asia. Singapore's Changi Airport (SIN) ranked 8th overall, followed by Jakarta's Soekarno-Hatta International Airport (CGK) in 10th place.

Kuala Lumpur International Airport (KUL), Hong Kong International Airport (HKG) and Bangkok's Suvarnabhumi International Airport (BKK) are also within the top 15 International megahubs.

11.3 Missing the Transfer Flight

11.3.1 Language Points and Useful Sentence Patterns

11.3.1.1 Language Points

1. on schedule

on time

2. wonder

if you wonder about something, you think about it, either because it interests you and you want to know more about it, or because you are worried or suspicious about it.

3. depart

when something or someone departs from a place, they leave it and start a journey to another place.

4. inform

if you inform someone of something, you tell them about it.

5. subsequent

we use subsequent to describe something that happened or existed after the time or event that has just been referred to.

6. take off

when an airplane takes off, it leaves the ground and starts flying.

7. alternate

we use alternate to describe a plan, idea, or system which is different from the one already in operation and can be used instead of it.

8. accommodate

to accommodate someone means to provide them with a place to live or stay.

9. get stuck

be unable to move further

10. shuttle bus

a bus that travels between two points

11.3.1.2 Useful Sentence Patterns

Asking for help

I have a connection to … Am I going to make it?
What should I do if I miss the connection?
I missed my connecting flight. What time does the next flight leave?

Have I missed my connection?

I think I missed my connecting flight.

I didn't arrive in time to make my connecting flight.

My flight was delayed so I couldn't get to my connecting flight on time.

Replies:

You'd better hurry up. Only … minutes left.

You'd better be hurry as time is limited.

Then you have to change your ticket.

The airline will provide you with overnight accommodations.

We will be responsible for your accommodation tonight.

We will provide a hotel room and some spending money.

Please have a complimentary dinner on us at the airport restaurant.

11.3.2 Dialogues

(A: Attendant   P: Passenger)

A: Excuse me, Madame. Did you press the call button?

P: Yes. It seems that we are unable to arrive on schedule, right?

A: Yes. I'm afraid so. There is a heavy thunderstorm ahead of us. We may arrive at the airport 40 minutes' delay.

P: Oh, I'm wondering whether I'll miss my connecting flight.

A: When does your connecting flight expect to depart?

P: An hour and a half later.

A: Don't worry, Madame. We will contact the ground staff immediately. You will be informed as soon as we get the information about your subsequent flight.

P: All right. Thanks a lot.

A: You are welcome.

(G: Ground Staff   P: Passenger)

P: Our flight was late, and I missed my connecting flight.

G: What's your flight number?

P: You mean the first flight I took?

G: No, the connecting flight.

P: It's CA 880.

G: Wait a moment, please. I'll check it for you.

P: OK.

G: Oh, yes. The connecting flight has taken off. We can help you find an alternate flight that will get you where you are going.

P: Whom should I call?

G: You are in the right place.

P: I think the flight we missed was the last flight out of here today.

G: We can go on the computer to try to find an alternate flight on another airline, if not, we can accommodate you.

P: What if I get stuck here and can't get out of this airport?

G: There is a shuttle bus that is still running and can take you into town to a hotel into the town.

P: I'm afraid I don't have enough money for a hotel room.

G: The flight that you missed is with our airline, so we will pay for your hotel room.

11.3.3 Cultural Background

Airport transfers cost more than flights

Holidaymakers spend more on airport transfers than flights to more than a third of European destinations, according to a new survey.

Research gathered by flight compensation company Flightdelays.co.uk found that the most expensive airport transfers were from Geneva, where the typical cost is £170, more than four times the cost of the average air fare from Manchester.

The next most expensive transfer is from Copenhagen, where passengers should expect to pay £170.67 for an average 10-mile journey to a hotel, compared to £50 for 617-mile flight from Manchester.

However, it is worth pointing out that the cost of the transfers might be shared between several passengers, which could bring per passenger the cost to below the typical air fare.

Flight delay claimed transfers from Belfast, Wheeze in Germany and Naples are also among the most expensive. The cheapest are from Milan and Moscow, it said.

The data analyzed the costs of all available airport transfer options, from rail travel to private car hire on June 1 to 80 different airports across popular destinations in Europe.

Costs were then compared with flights to the destinations on the same date.

Unit 12
Customs, Immigration and Quarantine

12.1　Going through Customs

12.1.1　Language Points and Useful Sentence Patterns

12.1.1.1　Language Points

1. declare

if you declare goods that you have bought in another country or money that you have earned, you say how much you have bought or earned so that you can pay tax on it

2. declaration form

a form that gives details of goods that have been brought into a country

3. article

a particular item or separate thing, especially one of a set

4. respectively

respectively means in the same order as the items that you have just mentioned

5. count

to include somebody/something when you calculate a total

6. personal

a personal opinion, quality, or thing belongs or relates to one particular person rather than to other people

7. belonging

the things that you own, especially things that are small enough to be carried

8. souvenir

a thing which you buy or keep to remind you of a holiday, place, or event

9. duty

duties are taxes which you pay to the government on goods that you buy

12.1.1.2　Useful Sentence Patterns

Asking questions

Have you read the customs form?

Will you show me your declaration form, please?

Have you finished filling out your declaration form?

Do you have anything to declare?

Anything special to declare?

What do you have in the suitcase?

What is/are this/these for?

Do I have to pay duty on this?

How much is the duty on this?

Replies:

Yes, I have.

Here you are.

I've filled in those items listed in the form.

Nothing. / No, I don't. / I have nothing to declare.

I have … to declare.

I just bought …

Everything in the suitcase is for my personal use.

This/These is/are … for …

They are my personal belongings.

You'll be charged duty for …

We'll have to charge you … on this.

12.1.2 Dialogues

(G: Ground Staff   P: Passenger)

G: Good morning, Sir. Can I help you?

P: Yes, please. This is my first time to go abroad. So I don't know what to declare and how to declare.

G: You have to fill in the declaration form before checking in.

P: But I don't know how to fill it in.

G: You have to name those articles with their price over 5,000 RMB respectively.

P: Should I write the number of pieces?

G: Yes. And you have to fill in your name, passport number and your destination.

P: Do I have to declare my iPhone?

G: Yes, your mobile phone counts.

P: All right. Thank you.

G: You may show it to that officer.

P: OK, I will.

G: Do you have anything to declare?

P: No. I just have some personal belongings.

G: Please show me your passport, declaration form and your baggage.

P: Here you are.

G: What are these?

P: These are souvenirs I bought in Korea for my friends.

G: And what about these two cameras?

P: I bought them in Korea, too. One is for personal use, and the other is for my son.

G: But you are allowed to have only one camera free of duty. So I'm afraid you have to pay duty for the second camera.

P: OK.

G: Do you have any other luggage?

P: No. The one you have checked is the only one.

G: Now you can go now.

P: Thank you.

12.1.3 Cultural Background

At the customs

At the customs, you should put all your luggage together, so that the customs officials can see clearly. Then remember several basic key words, for example, declare, duty free, dutiable, personal belongings, etc. Also remember several key sentences, such as, "Do you have anything to declare?" If you do not know clearly what should be declared, you may just say: "Could you tell me what have duty on them?" then the officials will help you.

The duty-free objects include several personal belongings. Here the word "several" refers to the quantities that the travelers need. As to some small gifts, if the price is low, they are duty-free. For example, the United States Customs allows the gifts that cost less than ＄10 duty-free. Fruit, vegetable, meat and meat product, live animals and addictable strong medicine, narcotic, etc. are all forbidden.

12.2 Going through Immigration

12.2.1 Language Points and Useful Sentence Patterns

12.2.1.1 Language Points

1. passport

an official document containing your name, photograph, and personal details, which you need to show when you enter or leave a country

2. tourist

a person who is visiting a place for pleasure and interest, especially when they are on holiday

3. visa

an official document, or a stamp put in your passport, which allows you to enter or leave a particular country

4. surprised

if you are surprised at something, you have a feeling of surprise, because it is unexpected or unusual

5. proceed

to continue to do something that has already been planed or started

6. purpose

your purpose is the thing that you want to achieve

7. sightseeing

if you go sightseeing or do some sightseeing, you travel around visiting the interesting places that tourists usually visit

8. return ticket

a ticket to a place and back (usually over the same route)

12.2.1.2 Useful Sentence Patterns

Asking questions

May I have …?

What is the purpose of your visit?

Where are you going to stay?

How long are you going to stay?

Can I have a look at your return ticket back to …?

How much money/foreign currency do you have with you?

Replies

Here you are. / Here it is. / Here is my …

I'm here for sightseeing/just for travelling/on vacation/on business/to visit…/to study.

I will stay at …

I'm going to stay for …

Yes, of course. Here it is.

About/Just …

12.2.2 Dialogues

(G: Ground Staff   P: Passenger)

G: May I have a look at your passport, please?

P: Sure.

G: You have a tourist visa. Where will you be staying?

P: Mainly in California.

G: I need to see your boarding pass.

P: Here you are.

G: Are you Chinese?

P: Yes.

G: There are quite a lot of Chinese people visiting right now.

P: I'm not surprised. Our school year just ended, and a lot of Chinese students are on vacation.

G: You're through now.

P: And what should I do then?

G: You may go to the baggage claim area and get your baggage, then proceed through the customs.

P: Thank you.

G: What is the purpose of your visit?

P: I visit here for sightseeing.

G: How long will you be staying in America?

P: About 15 days, I think.

G: Where are you staying during these days?

P: I'll stay at the Green Hotel.

G: Do you have a return ticket to Beijing?

P: Yes, of course.

G: It's all right. And how much money do you have with you?

P: I have about 3,000 U.S. dollars.

G: OK, you're through now.

P: Thank you very much.

12.2.3　Cultural Background

China's immigration and customs process bests US international airports

I'm on work travel that is taking me from my Washington DC base to Germany and China. Though I travel a lot, even I was amazed at the swiftness and friendly efficiency with which I was swept through immigration and customs at Frankfurt and Shanghai airports.

I'm signed on the US DHS' Global Entry/Trusted Traveler program, which is good…but I swear I still went through Frankfurt immigration quicker than I would have a hope of getting through Dulles, JFK and certainly LAX.

More surprising—the process was just as efficient at Shanghai, where a nice female immigration officer smiled, greeted me in English, scanned my passport, checked my visa and voila! After a barely-three-minute queue, hello China.

The US, meanwhile, greets its arriving passengers with waits that can easily be an hour or more, even though most documentation and information must be supplied in advance.

Worse, it has now permitted immigration and customs pre-clearance for travelers from Abu Dhabi to Washington Dulles to take place at Abu Dhabi airport (the way you are pre-cleared by US officers at Canada's airports). So those passengers arriving in the US can continue their journey straight from the plane as if it were a domestic flight, with no more inspections, while everyone else faces the tedious queues. The only carrier providing nonstop flights between those two points is Abu Dhabi's Etihad.

Either the US should take a note from other busy international airports such as Frankfurt and Shanghai (there are others that are highly efficient, including Hong Kong), and invest in more border control resources and better processing services, or it should extend pre-clearance to far more countries so they can enjoy equal status with Abu Dhabi.

12.3 Quarantine Inspection

12.3.1 Language Points and Useful Sentence Patterns

12.3.1.1 Language Points

1. on the spot

at the place in question; there

2. inspection

a formal or official examination

3. quarantine

if a person or animal is in quarantine, they are being kept separate from other people or animals for a set period of time, usually because they have or may have a disease

4. bureau

an office, organization, or government department that collects and distributes information

5. routine

we use routine to describe activities that are done as a normal part of a job or process

6. aquatic product

animals or plants lives or grows on or in water

7. confiscate

if you confiscate something from someone, you take it away from them, usually as a punishment

8. obey

if you obey a person, a command, or an instruction, you do what you are told to do

9. regulation

rules made by a government or other authority in order to control the way something is done or the way people behave

10. prohibit

if a law or someone in authority prohibits something, they forbid it or make it illegal

11. receipt

a piece of paper that you get from someone as proof that they have received money or goods from you

12. cooperate with

if you cooperate, you do what someone has asked or told you to do

13. import

to import products or raw materials means to buy them from another country for use in your own country

14. permit

an official document which says that you may do something

15. temporary

something that is temporary lasts for only a limited time

16. detainment

a state of being confined (usually for a short time)

12.3.1.2 Useful Sentence Patterns

Asking Questions

Do my pets need quarantine?

The healthy report, please?

We need the health report of your pet.

What is the procedure for importing plants?

How long will my pet be quarantined for?

Do they get all the required shots?

Replies

Your pet will need quarantine when entering the country.

There are specific importing requirements for plants.

Here you are./Here it is.

My dog is healthy and has got all the required shots.

The records of the vaccination are all on this paper.

12.3.2 Dialogues

(O: Official   T: Traveler)

O: Hello, is this luggage yours?

Unit 12 Customs, Immigration and Quarantine

T: Yes, it's mine.

O: I am the inspection and quarantine bureau. Please put the luggage on the belt of x-ray machine.

T: Why? There are films in my luggage. Will the machine damage them? What are you looking for on earth?

O: This is routine inspection. I promise x-ray machine will not damage your films.

T: Inspection again. I have no rights but to obey. I have no time to waste here.

O: Please open your box. What's in it?

T: Fruits, meat products and aquatic products. Any problem?

O: Yes, they must be confiscated.

T: Why? I am an American. You have no right to do things like this.

O: According to our laws, we have rights to do so. If you come to China, you must obey Chinese laws and regulations.

T: These plums are for my relatives in china. I promise there is nothing wrong with them.

O: There is great risk for fruits to carry and spread diseases and pests. No matter what these fruits are used for, they are prohibited from being brought into China by travelers.

T: What will you do after you confiscate them?

O: They will be sent to lab for further inspection and then be destroyed. Please leave all of the fruits, meat products and aquatic products here; please give me your passport. I need it to fill up the confiscation receipt.

T: You don't have to give me the receipt. It is of no use to me.

O: No matter whether you need it or not, I must give it to you. This is our regulation. Please cooperate with me.

T: Ok.

O: Sign here, please.

T: No problem.

O: Here is the receipt for you.

T: Thank you.

O: You are welcome.

O: Hello, gentleman. What's in your box?

T: Seedlings.

O: Have you brought seeds with you?

T: Yes. A pack of vegetable seeds and some flower seeds.

O: Please go to the inspection and quarantine office for declaration.

T: OK.

O: According to the relevant regulations, you must apply for the import permit in advance before you bring seeds or seedlings into china. Therefore, from now on we will keep these items for some time. You can take them away only after you finish going through all the formalities.

T: OK. I would like to accept your decision.

O: Thank you for your cooperation. And this is the receipt for temporary detainment.

12.3.3 Cultural Background

Quarantine inspection at the airport in Japan

There are many tourists travel to Japan and bring a lot of foods and fruits back to their countries. Do you know the quarantine inspection may be necessary when you take those groceries from Japan?

Each country established each policy and rules, and you have to follow and obey it when you get groceries into the country. The quarantine inspection determines whether it is not against a rule of your country or region first. And if they find nothing illegal they would issue permission and certificate to bring out from Japan. Afterwards, you have to pass through another quarantine inspection when you arrive at your country to make sure what you bring in is correctly written on the list of permission and sometimes you need to be checked again. The correspondence about fruits and plants that you are allowed to carry-on is varies each country and region. For example, a carry-on of most of fruits is prohibited except a few in Taiwan, quarantine dogs work for checking sometimes.

In addition, in some countries such as Australia, New Zealand and Thailand, you are allowed to bring back Japanese orange only when you have a proof of producing region, result of local quarantine and so on. On the other hand, immigration departments of Singapore and Malaysia don't establish such strict rules, allow you to bring in most of fruits without Japanese inspection.

This time we searched the rules of Hong Kong immigration, and found there is no rule and policy about this part. So you do not even need to be in Japanese quarantine. But in case you are asked about your belongings by immigration staff, you should answer to their questions politely because you do nothing wrong.

Know these rules as your knowledge, and enjoy your shopping more!

References

[1] 王晶，余明洋. 民航乘务英语听力[M]. 北京：国防工业出版社，2009.
[2] 《民航乘务英语》教材编写组. 民航乘务英语[M]. 北京：高等教育出版社，2006.
[3] 林扬，余明洋. 民航乘务英语视听[M]. 北京：旅游教育出版社，2014.
[4] 林扬. 民航乘务英语会话[M]. 4 版. 北京：旅游教育出版社，2017.
[5] 范建一. 民航乘务英语实用会话[M]. 北京：中国民航出版社，2004.
[6] 俞涛. 民航服务英语[M]. 北京：中国民航出版社，2011.
[7] 吴啸华，何蕾. 民航服务英语[M]. 北京：国防工业出版社，2017.
[8] 尹静. 民航地勤英语[M]. 北京：北京大学出版社，2008.
[9] 蒋焕新. 民航地勤服务英语[M]. 北京：科学出版社，2017.
[10] 王远梅. 空乘英语[M]. 北京：国防工业出版社，2010.
[11] 谢金艳，老青. 空乘及旅游英语视听说[M]. 北京：北京语言大学出版社，2014.
[12] 何志强. 民航客舱乘务英语[M]. 北京：中国民航出版社，2015.
[13] 林扬. 民航乘务英语会话[M]. 北京：旅游教育出版社，2007.
[14] 黎富玉. 民航空乘英语[M]. 北京：北京大学出版社，2008.
[15] 孙艳芬，孙楠楠. 民航服务英语[M]. 北京：高等教育出版社，2007.
[16] 俞涛. 民航服务英语[M]. 北京：中国民航出版社，2011.
[17] 张力，刘茗翀. 民用航空实务英语[M]. 北京：清华大学出版社，2016.
[18] 何志强. 民航客舱乘务英语[M]. 北京：中国民航出版社，2015.